SO
YOU
WANNA
TEACH,
HUH?

John Gauss, *1924-*

UNIVERSITY
PRESS OF
AMERICA

LANHAM • NEW YORK • LONDON

University Press of America, ® Inc.

4720 Boston Way
Lanham, MD 20706

3 Henrietta Street
London WC2E 8LU England

Printed in the United States of America

Library of Congress Cataloging in Publication Data

Gauss, John, 1924-
  So you wanna teach, huh?

  1. Teaching. 2. Classroom management. I. Title.
LB1025.2.G38   1985   371.1'02   85-5301
ISBN 0-8191-4629-3 (alk. paper)
ISBN 0-8191-4630-7 (pbk. : alk. paper)

All University Press of America books are produced on acid-free
paper which exceeds the minimum standards set by the National
Historical Publications and Records Commission.

This book is dedicated to my wife, Joyce, who helped and encouraged me in its writing.

SO YOU WANNA TEACH, HUH?

PREFACE

You must be thinking of becoming a school teacher or you would not be reading this book. Are you as puzzled as I was when I landed a teaching contract and could not find answers to my questions as to what to expect?

This book was written to smooth your way into the profession. It is not the ultimate word. Teaching is too elastic for that. Instead, this book is based on actual experience and is designed to give a glimpse into the inner mystique of teaching. Events cited in the book are the real world, not theory.

John Gauss

1 ‖ GET THE JOB FIRST

You're all set. You finished college and have a firm grip on that elusive teaching credential. All that remains is making the rounds of school districts to secure a teaching position. Right?

Wrong. You're too late. Someone else has the job.

LATE BIRDS GET WORMS

Nailing down teaching jobs in public school systems isn't done during the summer after graduation. Summer is vacation time for personnel directors, too, and they don't like to stick around doing interviews. They selected lineups for the fall semester long before your applications sailed across their doorsteps.

Submit your initial applications before January or as soon as you know you are going to graduate. Get them in early, before the mob, so you can be ready for interviews during the Easter/spring vacation.

That's hiring time. Plan on forgetting that outing to Fort Lauderdale or wherever. Work on getting your career launched. Jobs are never so plentiful that you can delay.

Principals want next year's schedule wrapped up well before the end of the present school year. They're anxious for summer vacation, and it's no contest if the choice is between talking to you and traveling in Europe.

Some principals moonlight on summer jobs. Your taking their precious time isn't going to result in an atmosphere favorable to your getting a teaching position.

MAKE YOUR BREAKS

Make looking for a teaching job your number one assignment during your college senior year. Devote the bulk of your time to it. Jobs won't come looking for you.

Research to find job openings. Ask friends in the school business. Janitors sometimes know of possible job openings before the school district personnel office. Ask college advisors. Check your college employment office. Locate county education offices in all sections of the country where you are willing to work (note that "willing to work" is not the same as "wanting to work"). Keep in touch with county education offices on a regular basis because they keep a file of available positions and job openings can appear at unexpected moments.

Call on various school districts in your county because each district does its own hiring. Visit other counties' education offices during Christmas vacation.

In the 1950's teachers could choose where and what they taught. It can happen again, but don't count on it. Work at getting the job. A surplus of teachers means scrambling to beat the competition for a toehold on the employment ladder. Former teachers who were dismissed because of lack of funds and/or students are anxious to leave car-parking jobs to return to the teaching arena.

Remember—they have priority and your name is far down the list. You have to put out extra effort.

THE BRIGHTER SIDE

There is good news if you are just now thinking of entering the teaching profession. The National Center for Education Statistics, a branch of the Education Department, looks forward to a need for teachers in the late 1980's after years of an oversupply.

According to its report, only seventeen percent of new college graduates majored in education in 1980 compared to

2

thirty-seven percent in 1970 and the number of new teacher graduates had dropped from 284,000 a year to 159,000. Yet, despite a decade of declining enrollments in elementary and secondary schools, the center predicts there will be more students in classrooms in 1990 than in 1970.

Even now, there is already a teacher shortage in science, mathematics, and agriculture. When prospective teachers were being turned away in droves in the late 1970's, I know of one person who returned to college and obtained a teaching degree in agriculture. Upon completion of requirements, this person had four immediate interviews resulting in four definite job offers at the high school level. He took a job teaching geography and agriculture in a school that was turning away geography teacher applicants.

GET THE NAME RIGHT

When you hear of a possible job opening, follow the lead immediately, but don't be in such a rush that you fail to learn the correct spellings and pronunciations of the names of the district superintendent and personnel director. This is *extremely* important.

Human nature being what it is, it upsets people when their names are misspelled or mispronounced. It might seem silly to you, but people become irrational. I know of an applicant who greeted the personnel director with an incorrect name over the telephone. His impending interview was cancelled with no explanation.

Another practical reason for learning the correct name is the unbelievable number of ways people say and spell their names. When you teach, you'll struggle with this fact.

I once observed a woman who, while enrolling her son in kindergarten, gave the son's name to the clerk as "Gooie." She had bestowed the name on her newborn after reading a novel. Asked to spell the name, she spelled "G-U-Y."

Telephone the school district and ask a clerk the name of

the current personnel director. Ask to have it spelled. It's time well spent.

APPLY YOURSELF

Go to each school district office and *personally* ask for an application blank. Why bother when you could simply write or telephone? Because it makes you a familiar face next time you walk through the doorway. Stop to chat with the personnel secretary if she's not busy. Ask about any special needs the school district has for teachers. Making a good impression on the secretary won't hurt your chances. Your application could end up closer to the top of the stack. It might be quite a heap of papers because large districts receive thousands of applications. I remember a school district's receiving several hundred applications for each available job even back in the 1960's when teachers were more in demand.

Fill in the application neatly. That's *neatly*. Silly that it's mentioned? I've talked to many secretaries about the number of messy, misspelled applications crossing personnel desks. It cuts down your competition unless your application is among the messy ones. A messy, poorly done application only serves to produce a few laughs in the office.

Check your birthdate. It might seem obvious that birthdate means the day, month, and year of your birth. Some college graduates have trouble with the obvious. Lots of your competition will melt away because applicants wrote the present year as part of the birthdate. Don't join the group. It's good for another laugh at the personnel office.

Take time with each of several dozen applications you send. You read it right. Several dozen. It's a dream world you live in if you think applications to one or two places will do the trick. Some districts won't reply and you'll be wasting valuable time.

BE PERSONAL

Fill in each application in ink in your best handwriting. Maybe you're the best typist in the city, but personnel people like the personal touch. They want to know you can write. Complete all blanks. Draw a line in any space not applicable to you. A blank spot generates doubt about whether it was intentional or not. Make photocopies of applications for your files, but *do not* send a photocopy. Send the original. Make each application fit job openings in the district if you know of available positions.

Write a good cover letter. A cover letter is a letter telling complete strangers what your mother used to tell to all who would listen. What she told when she was bragging about you, that is. Mention your desire to teach and why it would benefit the district to hire you. The cover letter can be typed and must not be a form letter. Make it appear as though you have a personal interest in the particular school district. It's wise not to overkill so your cover letter, which is sent along with the application, should not be too sweet. Naturally, you keep a copy and send the original.

Keep the cover letter short. One page is the maximum length and a few short paragraphs is better. Proofread the letter and your application. Have someone else read it for mistakes. Another pair of eyes is always better for finding errors. Remember, one error and you're out. Baseball allows you three strikes, not prospective employers.

BACKUP YOUR BACKGROUND

Type a resume. Take time to do it right. Check out a resume book from the library or buy one. They're plentiful and easy to find. There is no one correct way to write a resume. Use a style that suits you. Again, be neat. Be accurate. Don't omit positive factors in your background. Do omit or barely mention negative factors.

The resume gives you an opportunity to stress your employment history. Give all dates of employment and play up any work—even volunteer, unpaid work—that makes you look more attractive to a prospective employer. If any job was temporary, say so. Don't create doubts about why you were terminated.

Use short paragraphs and include all facts making you appear to be a desirable employee. Mention the Bible class you lead, or how you were an active summer camp leader. Any activity relating to youngsters or any interest in a possible subject area helps your image and your employment chances. One teacher I know was hired because of a hobby in photography. School principals like variety.

Many people make the mistake of having only one resume. Be flexible. Write several resumes, each geared to a particular area. If you majored in physical education and minored in English and music, make three separate resumes. In one emphasize your background in sports and your letters earned in high school and college. In another emphasize English and in a third place the emphasis on music. Do be sure to mention all three backgrounds in all three resumes, but use a different slant for each one. The more varied your background, the better your chances of securing a teaching position.

School districts want people who can step into more than one position. They *need* qualified persons who can fill different slots in the schedule. Ask any high school coach how many times he or she has been given a classroom assignment to teach math, history, biology, or what have you. The assignment didn't even have to be in the coach's area of knowledge. Teachers are moved about to meet schedule needs. The more versatility your resume indicates, the better reception it will receive.

Your resume should be returned with the completed application blank. *Proofread all resumes* before mailing.

FOLLOW THROUGH

A common fault of many people after sending resumes and applications is sitting back and staring at the telephone until it rings with news of a job offer. It could be a long wait.

Do a follow-up. Check in personally at districts after a suitable wait of a few weeks. Don't ask about your application. Just drop in to inquire about any openings coming up in the future. Be friendly. It will help office personnel to remember your face and your name.

Avoid getting in the way or loitering. Also, don't overdo and drop in *every* week. This puts you in the pest classification and your folder will find a permanent niche under the application pile. One or two visits spaced well apart should be enough.

Don't have the time? Use the telephone. A friendly call is a poor substitute for a personal visit, but it is preferable to a silent wait at home.

JOHNNY-ON-THE-SPOT

If all efforts seem in vain, there's still hope. Teachers are human. Plans change. Drop in at all personnel offices on your list of prospects *the first week of September.* Yes, I know. All hiring was done in the spring. But teachers don't always tell the district office they aren't returning.

Teachers frequently fail to report for work in the fall. A spouse secures a job in another city, a sudden illness becomes serious, or the battle of the classroom makes retirement quite attractive, and, unexpectedly, there's a position open in September. Many—repeat—many personnel directors take the first qualified person walking through the doorway when hit with this common situation. Hiring the first available body is easier than wading through the stack of applications and contacting applicants. Personnel people have been known to hire teachers who never sent in an application but were standing in the office when a job opening suddenly occurred.

Schools sometimes incorrectly anticipate their needs. No school ever knows exactly how many students to expect the first day of school. Occasionally more students enroll than the school envisioned when hiring teachers. Frequently this means hiring additional staff after school starts. You could be lucky. Be available.

THE INTERVIEW

Maybe several school districts nibble at the bait of your resume and schedule interviews. Usually personnel offices do an initial screening interview and then send applicants to a school to be interviewed by the principal or, more commonly in these days of teacher involvement, by a committee of teachers and a principal.

It's the first impression that counts. You might never get a second lookover. Be at ease. Impossible? Of course it is. No one's at ease during interviews—not even interviewers. The trick is to appear calm. Sit well back in the chair, feet not crossed, hands relaxed. Wear conservative, not somber, clothing. Avoid extreme fashions. Women should avoid heavy eye shadow and makeup. Men usually do better when clean shaven. Beards still have less than total acceptance. Men can always grow a beard after the job is secured. Nobody will be fired for having one, but get the job first.

The interview is your one and only chance. Prepare yourself. Be ready to ask questions about the district and the position open. Show lively interest. Be enthusiastic. Be ready to tell how you can benefit the school. Offer suggestions about getting the utmost from students in your future classes. Be sincere; be friendly; be outgoing. Most people are hired and retained on the basis of personality. Make yours show through during the interview. Your resume has already told them about your qualifications. Your background's acceptable or you would not be there. Interviewers now want to judge your enthusiasm for teaching.

Don't worry about health plans, retirement, or teaching conditions. Later, after paychecks are coming regularly, you can join the union and fight for fringe benefits, but first get a job. These days most districts have good extra benefits and you'll be told of them when you sign a contract to teach.

BE A SUBSTITUTE

What if September rolls around and you're still washing dishes at Greasy Diner? Don't despair. All is not lost.

Get your name placed on the substitute lists of local school districts. All districts need substitutes. Teaching is a high-risk situation. Imagine yourself sealed within a room with twenty to thirty-five youngsters who cough in your air space, itch with ringworm, and give you papers to read after rubbing pinkeye infections with their hands. Cold and flu epidemics hit teachers as soon as the first student becomes ill. Thus, there's a great need for substitutes.

As a substitute you can expect early morning calls to report to work at distant schools to teach unfamiliar topics to unknown youngsters. Substitutes can turn down jobs, but don't turn down too many. Being dependable and being able to substitute at a variety of grade levels increases your income and your chances of landing a regular position. Substitutes refusing many jobs find themselves employed only during epidemics.

So why expose yourself to possible illness, unruly youngsters, and uncertain employment? The pay isn't that great. Substitutes are paid far below minimum teachers' salaries.

As a substitute you'll be a known personality. You enter schools and become familiar with the inner workings of an entire district. Principals will know you. You will hear workroom gossip telling of a teacher's quitting before the personnel office knows of it. When a position occurs, you'll be on the spot with recognized qualifications. It's human nature to hire someone who is known. Why else is nepotism so common?

It's just possible that you will be called upon to substitute on a long-term basis. Teachers do become ill or have accidents requiring convalescence for the remainder of the year. Long-time substitutes don't get regular teacher's pay, but do have an advantage if the teacher resigns. If the principal likes the way you handle the class, hiring you is an easy way out for the district.

BEWARE OF PITFALLS

There are a few situations to avoid when seeking a teaching position. Graft and corruption are extremely rare in school districts, but not unknown. If anyone suggests you can easily have a teaching position if a school board member was to receive a sum of money, run—don't walk—to the nearest exit. As mentioned, it is extremely rare because the average school board member is an honest, dedicated person with a sincere interest in education, so it's unlikely you will be faced with the issue. If you did succumb to such an offer, you wouldn't be happy. Any such district would be ridden with other problems that would make teaching unpleasant.

Another rare, but less so, problem is for a personnel man to make lewd implications hinting that if a female applicant was more friendly, a teaching position could be obtained. Don't fall into the trap. Get the job on your ability to teach, nothing else. Such personnel men don't last long, and when they leave, there's a cloud of suspicion over the heads of persons they've hired.

Another, and unfortunately common, pitfall is not having a teaching credential *the day you start teaching*. It is your responsibility to have a teaching credential. I know of several teachers who assumed the school district would follow through and see that the credential was issued and on file with the county education office. They assumed wrong and were not paid. Remember, a school district cannot legally pay anyone not credentialed by the state in which they teach. No teaching credential, no paycheck. It's that simple. Why work for nothing?

TAKE A SHORTCUT

Perhaps you are just beginning to think of being a teacher. Good. This book can open the eyes of any misty-eyed idealist. Maybe you have a college degree, but want to pick up a teaching credential. If so, you might be able to save some time.

I met a discouraged, married college grad who had quit his job and returned to college to acquire a teaching credential. His discouragement came not from being married, but by the two-year program his college required before it would grant a teaching credential. He was ready to drop out of college.

Fortunately, we talked it over first. As a result he was teaching six months later when the fall semester began. How? By learning one simple fact. Teaching credentials are issued by the state, not by colleges. Colleges only recommend. His college, like so many others, set up the two-year course of study with excessive requirements.

My suggestion was for him to seek out the county education office and have them evaluate his college courses already taken as compared to the list of requirements from the state. He did so and found he needed only three additional courses to qualify for a teaching credential, not a two-year program. He finished the necessary courses, applied directly to the state for his credential and had a teaching position secured when the credential arrived. Naturally, he had applied for the job as soon as he knew he would receive a credential. Waiting would have delayed him another year.

Examine all possibilities. It might be easier to become a teacher than you think. School districts do need and hire replacement teachers every school year. Why shouldn't you be one of those hired?

2 ‖ BEGINNING YOUR YEAR RIGHT

When the elation of landing a teaching contract wears off, the shock of reality hits like a cloudburst on a summer day. You asked for it, but are you ready? What's next? Have years spent listening to college professors prepared you for the real world? Probably not. A wide gulf exists between doing college assignments and having the sole responsibility for a classroom.

BARE WALLS AND BLANK MIND

Stepping into your own classroom for the first time is unsettling. All those desks—each soon to be occupied! Is there any space not filled with desks? Can you handle so many youngsters? And those empty, blank walls. They must be covered. Can you ever make attractive bulletin boards? This is a lonely, depressing moment when you wonder what have you let yourself in for. You feel like a stranger with nowhere to turn for help.

Fortunately, there's a way out besides immediately resigning. Don't panic yet. You have all year and lots of opportunities to do that.

PRESCHOOL ANGUISH WEEK

School district leaders, understanding the difficult transition from summer vacation to the battle of teaching unwilling youngsters, plan a week of preschool activities— usually consisting of meetings so boring that teachers give thanks when school actually starts.

13

During the week prior to the opening of school expect to have lots of meetings—dull, dull meetings. The first of many during the school year, I might add. Get used to them. You could be that rare person who actually finds such meetings enjoyable.

Smaller districts generally have one glad-you're-all-back meeting where you'll feel out of place as returning teachers—never refer to them as *old* teachers—greet each other with restrained enthusiasm. They don't want to be there either.

A few districts plan an earlier breakfast meeting just for beginning teachers several days before a general district meeting. At least, they did when districts were hiring teachers by the gross. With fewer hirings these days this early get-acquainted meeting is not as common as in former years. If you have such a meeting, it can ease the strain of newness as you meet other newly-hired teachers. Possibly you'll strike up friendships so you'll have people to talk with when the district has a larger, general meeting for all district personnel.

Most of the largest school districts now omit general district meetings because of difficulties involved in squeezing thousands of bodies into one area without chaos. In these districts, superintendents sometimes give pep talks on television. Teachers are expected to listen. Sometimes they do—especially when mandatory attendance in front of a school television set is required.

Feel fortunate if your district omits general meetings. Or maybe you like group singing, dull speeches and introductions of school board members. If so, you'll have a thrilling morning.

STRANGE FACES AND HOPE

Faculty meetings will be held at your school during this preschool week and you'll find yourself either wedged into a student-sized desk in a classroom or sitting in a cafeteria. Expect to be introduced. Expect also to have a sea of blank

14

faces introduced to you if yours is a small school. Don't despair. You'll associate names and faces in time. Just be on the lookout for a friendly face. This will be a person you can latch on to after the meeting.

Unlike general district meetings, faculty meetings are important to you. It's your chance to learn. Soak up information. Ask questions. Returning teachers know the ropes and forget that newcomers struggle with the morass of simple details. Principals tend to gloss over matters so important to a beginner. So make your questions known. Speak up even when you think your question is stupid. Teachers understand. They went through the same qualms.

Use faculty meetings to your advantage. Latch on to every bit of information bandied about. Much can be learned from casual conversations among returning teachers. Listen and ask questions. You won't lose face. Teachers are used to ignorance. It's what puts money in their pockets. Learn every bit of daily routines that must be an ingrained part of your working day. Later this information will be passed on to students, and that's when you'll lose face if you don't know answers.

WHERE'S THE RESTROOM?

Leave these faculty meetings with enough basic knowledge to launch you on your career. At least, have enough information to get you through the first day.

If not, seek that teacher who gave you a friendly smile at the faculty meeting. Ask this person the questions you were reluctant to ask at the meeting—things like locations of restrooms, faculty restrooms. If you teach in a grammar school, using children's facilities could cramp your back, and using student facilities in any school tends to be inhibiting.

Ask about supplies. Some schools have an open supply room where teachers freely take what they need when they need it. Other schools assign a person to control supplies and set fixed times to obtain items. Sometimes schools will assign the school secretary to handle certain materials, let the custodian control other items, and place an art teacher in charge of craft or bulletin board supplies. Check it out while you have a chance. You won't have the opportunity after students begin their year.

TAKE A HIKE

Take time also to walk around the school. Note locations of student restrooms, lunch benches, the nurse's office, the cafeteria, student bicycle racks, bus loading areas and other places. In junior or senior high schools notice locations of gyms and dressing rooms. Be sure you know which is for boys and which is for girls. You'll be asked where these places are. Students are filled with questions and expect teachers to be all-knowing.

Some schools have a special teachers' dining room. Find it. Learn the prices of lunches. Determine whether teachers pay a different price than students. They usually do.

Notice the locations of fire extinguishers. Learn the signal for fire drills and the procedure for taking your class outside. Schools have monthly fire drills, and if you thrill to being in the limelight, just take a boisterous class in the wrong direction during one of these drills.

Locate the workroom or faculty lounge. Some schools have both. You can easily locate these rooms by the cigarette smoke and bursts of laughter drifting down hallways. These are the social watering holes—for coffee— and waste some time here getting to know your fellow workers. After school begins the workroom becomes just that, a place for working. Here is where the wornout typewriter and duplicator from the school office are deposited for teachers' use. Much of your school year outside your classroom will be spent in the workroom.

BE PREPARED

By now you'll begin to feel at home at school. Slip into your classroom and take time to think. Get materials ready for the first day of school. Go over the procedure for registering students. Do you need forms to fill out? Get them. Should you have pencils ready? Paper? A roll book? What about the class seating arrangement? Should you rearrange desks? Will you need a seating chart? Are you ready to give directions to the nurse's office? The cafeteria? What's the procedure for students who enter late? Do you now understand school regulations enough to pass the information to students? Negative answers better send you scurrying to that friendly teacher for answers.

WORK IT OUT

Now is the time to plan the first week in detail. Your principal should have given you general information concerning your assignment. Some don't. My first teaching assignment is clearly etched in my mind. The principal guided me to a room bare of books and supplies, handed me a pupil's history textbook and informed me I was to teach math, history and English. No books would be available for months. Planning how to teach was my responsibility. You should be luckier.

A few schools have detailed outlines for teachers to follow, but most use only general guidelines and give teachers lots of elbow room. Three teachers teaching the same subject in the same school will never be teaching in the same manner. You're allowed to be quite flexible. Like the captain of a ship, you are in complete charge of your classroom. You receive some of the praise and all the blame for whatever happens within your room. Make lesson plans that take advantage of your unique teaching methods.

Make a good workable plan for each hour of the first teaching week. Allow for every minute. The worst blunder in teaching is having idle students. Write your lessons in a plan book to be available for substitutes, but don't be naive and think you will follow them to the letter. Allow for flexibility. Nothing goes according to plan around children. Prepare so you are organized enough to feed blocks of information to your students in doses they can absorb. Good preparation builds your confidence by placing you one step ahead of the students.

Make a sketchy plan for the year. Don't bother with much more than a general outline of your goals. Until the end of the first teaching day you won't know how many pupils you'll have or what their levels of ability are. When you know these, then plan for the year. For now, be content to last the first week.

DRESS IT UP

After planning your first week and giving thought to the balance of the year, give room appearance some attention.

Cover bulletin boards with bright, light colors. Use large pictures and short headings or titles. Children at the back of the room appreciate seeing pictures, too. Besides, large pictures take more space. Cut out letters for captions or write them. Writing is faster. Primary grade teachers letter captions in a style taught at their grade level. Some teachers buy commercial letters, but I find these too stilted. Handmade letters look friendlier.

Don't waste too much time on bulletin boards. The idea is for the first impact upon students to be pleasant. After the first day nobody notices bulletin boards again until you change them. I've never bothered hiding spelling words which were on bulletin boards during spelling tests. One student out of thirty might remember they're there.

Develop a bulletin board theme. Back-to-school is reliable. It's also over-used. Use a general theme that won't need changing every week when you're bogged down with daily assignments. Working on bulletin boards assumes low

18

priority when students crowd your desk. Plan to have at least one bulletin board for student displays. All students need the satisfaction of seeing their work shown in public. Elementary school teachers do this routinely, but sometimes junior and senior high teachers forget how important it is.

Displaying student work not only fills in space on blank walls, it also makes your task easier. I've seen students change for the better after a quiet pat on the back—by way of displaying their work, of course. It puffs up their importance in their own eyes. Every student excels in at least one assignment. Find and display it. If a student appears to lack any skill worthy of being displayed, consider a special project just for that person.

BEG OR BORROW

Barren of ideas for decorating the classroom? Check with other teachers. Returning teachers often keep old bulletin board material because teachers are born pack rats. It's possible you can borrow something useful to cover those blank walls. It doesn't take an art major to slap a couple of interesting pictures on a bulletin board.

I've seen teachers settle for an up-to-date calendar and a chart or two on the wall in junior and senior high schools. It is not recommended. Have stimulating, eye-catching displays. Cold-appearing rooms add to teaching difficulties. Don't create problems. Create a pleasant atmosphere.

ORGANIZED CHAOS

The first day is hectic! When students surge into your room you'll know how Custer felt as he counted the Indians. Unlike Custer, you'll possibly survive. Be calm. Although it's no consolation to you, all returning teachers share your emotions. Years of service is no preparation for the shock.

Expect the unexpected. Two pupils to each desk? Don't worry. Dump the problem in the principal's lap. Just be certain that every pupil in the room is assigned there. Send all strays to the proper room or the office.

Take roll very carefully. Take your time to do it right. *This is important.* The school must account for every student. Be accurate. Spell all names correctly. At upper grade levels be on the lookout for students changing the legal spelling of their names. Match a face to every name. Do not record names in your permanent roll book yet. Wait a week until latecomers are added to your class and all assignment mistakes are corrected. It's even possible you will be reassigned to another classroom or teaching position after all pupils in the school are sorted out. It happened to me several times.

THREE THINGS

You will want to accomplish three things the first day. First, as mentioned, obtain an accurate roll of the class. Say each name aloud and check spelling and pronunciation. Never assume students pronounce their names as you would.

Second, set standards for the year. Let students know what you expect them to learn. Explain precisely what materials they should bring to class each day. Impress upon them the boundaries of behavior. Set rules the class and you can follow during the year. Once you set a rule, stick to it. Children operate better under a well-disciplined, fair routine. Don't be rough. Be constant. Students do their utmost with fair-minded, organized teachers.

The third accomplishment that first day is to leave school with an initial feeling of class levels. Every class has a collective personality. What do your students already understand? How readily can they assimilate new offerings? How firm must control be? The faster you know, the more effective and relaxed you will be. Teachers having several classes a day recognize that each class is different. It's not uncommon to teach the same subject to six classes a day using different materials and methods for each group. You must adjust to your classes. To do otherwise will create problems you don't need.

THE LONG HAUL

Real work begins the second day. Students, believe it or not, are anxious to learn. It won't last. Foster it. Don't kill enthusiasm with dull, uninspiring assignments. The longer you maintain their enthusiasm, the more effective your results will be.

Use part of the first week discussing school regulations with students. Explain reasons for rules they question. Why can't they run in the hallways? Is gum chewing not allowed? Why? Explain in terms they understand.

After your first few teaching years when you have witnessed accidents and have removed sticky gum from your clothing and books, you'll be better able to interpret the rules to your classes. As a beginner, explain as well as you can. You will be expected to enforce all school regulations whether you personally believe in them or not. Don't tell students if you don't like a school rule. Seek to change the regulation during faculty meetings.

Give students other information needed to function. Mention lunch procedure, fire drill procedure, and library procedure. Returning students usually know the information, but you will have several students new to the school. They need to know the regulations and procedures and it doesn't hurt to tell all students again. This prevents their using the alibi of not understanding rules.

TESTS AND MORE TESTS

Usually part of the first week is spent testing students. Some school districts use standardized diagnostic tests in certain grade levels. These are helpful if your district requires them. Unfortunately, it sometimes take weeks to get the results if the grading is out of your hands. You need to know student ability levels immediately to eliminate wasted motion and time.

Devise your own testing procedure. It doesn't have to be elaborate. Determine what you want to know about your class and make a simple, easy-to-grade test. Make several tests if necessary. Keep them short. The idea is to keep students busy the first few days until your class is completed with added newcomers and at the same time get an understanding of what you will be able to teach. Then you can really get rolling the second week without confusion.

Students are eager to know the results of their tests. Use your own judgment about whether to tell them. If you do, do it individually. Avoid announcing results to the entire class unless you generalize. The purpose of testing is having test scores as a basis for planning the year's lessons and telling a student about a low score might cause feelings of failure, while telling a student about a high test score might cause the student to relax and believe it's not necessary to study.

Explain to older students that the purpose of the diagnostic tests is to find their present educational level so you can plan the year's program to suit them. They'll understand. Never give a test unless you contemplate a use for it. There's not enough time in a school year to teach everything you plan, so why waste time?

OH, NOT AGAIN

Interruptions! Teaching is one interruption after another. That's why you have to remain flexible. Take interruptions in stride.

The first week might see a flow of students being transferred to and from your class. You'll have students leaving lunches and personal belongings in the room and returning to fetch them if you have more than one class. The office will send memorandums to your room by student helpers so frequently you will think you have a swinging door. You'll have interruptions within the class. Students will want to get a drink of water or leave to use the restroom. They'll drop pencils and books or demand answers to silly questions when you explain lessons. Expect it. It's all part of the business. Nobody said it would be easy.

Expect interruptions all year. They'll happen in the middle of tests, films, class discussion and at all inopportune times. Parents will drop in and demand your immediate attention. The principal will walk in unannounced. An unexpected assembly will occur. Pupils will be called from the room to practice for the Thanksgiving play. Interruptions happen frequently.

One interruption I recall from my first year of teaching was a sudden fire drill. It was the best and fastest drill I ever witnessed. A junior high student, in the principal's office prior to his being suspended from school, became bored by a heated discussion between his parents and school authority, so he wandered to the fire alarm box and pressed the control. Bells rang and the entire school promptly filed outside. His parents thought it was a great joke. Years later I read in the newspapers about his being sentenced to state prison for robbery. I wonder if his parents thought that was a joke, too.

THE BRIGHT SIDE

Don't despair if interruptions destroy your high goals and expectations. Look on the bright side. Next week you can use any lesson plan you didn't finish the first week. You'll be ahead of the game.

There's always next week. Beginning teachers frequently have vague, uneasy feelings on Sunday. Monday is coming. No matter how exciting the weekend activities, the following week must be planned. A leftover plan from the previous week is always helpful.

To ease your mind Sunday nights, stay at school a few extra minutes on Fridays. Leaving a carefully planned lesson on

23

your desk for Monday makes Sunday more enjoyable. Then, too, if you have so much weekend fun that a substitute has to face your class on Monday, you'll be more relaxed.

3 ‖ FELLOW EMPLOYEES

Unless you teach in a one-room or two-room schoolhouse, there will be a group of behind-the-scenes workers around the campus. These are non-teaching people who make your job smoother. Gone are the days when teachers had to do everything from chopping wood to making student pens. Make it your business to become acquainted with these people. It'll make teaching easier.

THE PHANTOM OF THE CAMPUS

Somewhere an elusive person lurks within the maze of cubicles comprising the average school. Like the famed Phantom of the Opera, he exists but seldom surfaces into view. Possibly you might catch a rare glimpse of him rounding a far corner of a building or disappearing mysteriously into a hidden recess. To you he is the most important person in the entire school. Track him down the first day you set foot on the school grounds. Find him. Cultivate him. Become his friend. Your life as a teacher will be more fruitful.

Who is this person of such importance? Are we thinking of the chief administrator? Perish the thought. The school principal will never achieve this person's ability to make your teaching life pleasant.

It is the school custodian, the janitor, whom you must track down and greet warmly. In districts that reward labor with titles, not money, the custodian might be called a building superintendent or maintenance engineer. Whatever the title, become a friend.

GO HUNTING

This man or, occasionally, woman shuns the limelight. He remains on the outskirts of education waiting to be given tasks. In any given school, several small, unnoticed, undetected cubbyholes are sprinkled between restrooms, under stairways, behind boiler rooms or in basements. These are the custodian's treasured spaces. Here he can be located amid cleaning implements and strong-smelling fluids.

Located, that is, if you have the determination of a big game hunter seeking the last white rhino on earth. Trapping him nears the impossible, but, like a wild animal making morning rounds to water holes, the custodian does have a routine. No matter how difficult, discovering his daily method of operation is worth all effort.

WISE VERSUS FOOLISH TEACHERS

Wise teachers on good terms with the custodian find ordinary activities running more smoothly, but in times of stress they find the custodian's friendship invaluable. Teachers knowing the custodian's haunts can dispatch student messengers at odd times of the day to summon instant aid.

Minor annoyances are always being faced in the classroom. Bolts and screws apparently dissolve causing the collapse of desks, doors, window fasteners, and room fixtures. A friendly janitor remedies the situation immediately. Paint spilled on the floor? A student lunch regurgitated over your desk and shoes? No problem. The custodian appears with his faithful mop. The pencil sharpener disintegrates? New parts quickly have it grinding again.

You will find a few foolish teachers who scorn janitors as persons unworthy of attention. They grudge a quick nod of recognition or a happy birthday greeting once a year. These souls are forever struggling with broken faucets and rickety desks. Custodians are busy people. They file notes pleading for help until there is a free moment. Free moments are sometimes scarce. It could take days before a broken roller on a wall map is mended. Not surprisingly, friendlier teachers gain attention much quicker.

BRING FLOWERS

Another fellow employee worthy of note is the school secretary. Unlike the custodian, she is easily found. Look in the office and you'll see her figuratively chained to her desk. Most secretaries manage to remain pleasant under grueling conditions and constant interruptions. They intercept the initial shock of irate citizens walking into school offices or telephoning in highly emotional states. They absorb much anger directed at the school and calm agitated parents before they visit you.

Be nice to the secretary. Bring her flowers and forget her birthday. Say nice things about her new outfit. Tell her your appreciation when she does something for you. She deserves your praise. Secretaries make the school hum. Your school secretary will have tabs on situations long before word filters down to you.

The secretary reminds you of deadlines of those countless reports. She passes messages to you when your spouse or lover calls to remind you to pick up a can of beans on the way home from work. She patiently shows the novice how to operate ancient duplication devices found in educational institutions. She quietly corrects misspelled words in notices you give her to print in daily bulletins.

Secretaries worth their salt put in a full day for little pay. So nod greetings to her in the morning. Chat briefly with her about her children. Be pleasant, but don't infringe upon her time. Chances are she is frantically trying to meet a paper deadline.

However, do feel free to discuss your problems relating to the school if it's in her responsibility area. Allow lots of time if it's a favor you're asking. Asking her to duplicate two hundred

27

copies of a lesson you intend giving to your class that day is too much to expect. She can't do the impossible.

THE TIGHTROPE WALKER

Doing the impossible is the job of the school principal, the chief administrator. Every school has a boss and the principal is it. Like a circus performer, the principal balances on a tight wire juggling the desires of school superintendents, board members, parents, pupils, and teachers. One mistake and the principal is banished to the Siberia of all school administrators, the classroom. Principals are former teachers who worked hard to leave the classroom and most of them will work harder to stay out, especially since it means a lower salary. As a teacher you should be warned that you are the expendable ball in the juggling act. If the principal's act slips because of your actions, you will be the fall guy.

SCHEDULING WOES

A principal is responsible for the working schedule so stay on his or her good side. You, as a first-year teacher, should not expect a cream-of-the-crop assignment. Sometimes, given the number of available rooms, teachers, and students, unbelievable schedules are developed. I have found myself skipping between several rooms during the day, lugging necessary supplies along in a basket. I have found myself and another teacher teaching in the same room at the same time, have found myself without a scheduled lunch, have taught mathematics in art and music rooms, and have taught in rooms undergoing remodeling. These are all woes of scheduling. Scheduling the principal does.

SPEAK UP

Principals make schedules that are expedient—that is, expedient to themselves. If you are stuck with a schedule Superman couldn't follow, talk with the principal. Sometimes there's an easy solution. I have had my teaching schedule adjusted several times simply by switching classes or classrooms with another teacher. A minor flaw in the schedule was settled satisfactorily before creating year-long frustrations. The principal just hadn't noticed the problem. Sometimes there is no satisfactory solution. An overcrowded school can cause massive scheduling headaches.

If you find yourself skipping from room to room every year or always being stuck with the school's behavior problems, speak to the principal. He has his own problems and tends to overlook yours.

Poorer assignments should be rotated. Expect your share, especially the first few years, but don't be caught short every year. Grab your share of good years, too.

BIG BROTHER

A good principal can make your teaching career quite enjoyable. He can guide you over rough spots, give valuable advice, and administer quick aid with classroom control.

The principal also is responsible for evaluating your teaching ability and helping you improve your teaching techniques.

Principals order supplies and can block orders for supplies you think you need. They determine who will teach what to whom. They get the brunt of callers who think schools are poorly run, ill-disciplined, and train children to be public nuisances. Principals sometimes field calls and keep irate parents off your back.

It is possible you will find yourself working with a principal who is not top-notch. People are raised to positions where they are incompetent in education as in other fields. If you find yourself assigned to a principal you simply cannot tolerate, transfer to another school as fast as you can. Conditions are not likely to improve for you. If, after transferring to another school, you're still having run-ins with your principal, carefully consider your own personality quirks. Nobody's perfect.

THE SCHOOL VICE

Larger schools have a vice-principal. The vice-principal, not the principal, tackles discipline cases in schools and it is to the VP that you will send unruly students. Talk to the VP if a student is giving you a bad time. Trouble might be averted. Some tips on maintaining discipline in your classroom to ease the burden on your and the VP's shoulders are included in the next chapter.

The vice-principal has charge of the school when the principal is away and sometimes does pupil or teacher scheduling, teacher evaluations, and pupil control during lunch and at bus stops.

Much of the VP's time is spent waiting for the principal to retire. He longs to step into the principal's shoes and avoid handling all those major student-discipline problems.

FIRST AID

Find the school nurse. It's not always easy. She might not be in her office. She might not even be on the school grounds. Schools have a school nurse on call, but she is frequently assigned to more than one school. Sometimes there's not a registered nurse on duty and a nurse's aid is on call. She might not be as qualified as a regular nurse.

Nurses are not doctors. They do not treat patients. Nurses can do necessary first aid, but their help is restricted. They do not give any medication, even aspirin for headaches, without a doctor's orders. They do keep medication on hand for students who bring it to school and must take the prescribed medication during the day.

So why a nurse? What do they do? A school nurse can be a great help to you. If you teach long enough, you will, as I have, be overseeing students who have lost an eye or a limb, or have severe emotional problems. You'll witness students undergoing epileptic seizures or the brief memory loss of petit mal. A chat with the nurse can enlighten you and allow you to adjust to situations.

Bothered by body odor—a pupil's, not yours? Let the nurse talk to the pupil. It saves the pupil from being embarrassed by a teacher one has to face every day. Any embarrassed student is a non-learning student. You'll have enough of those without creating more.

A student suddenly becomes ill as you hand out test questions? It's a quick trip to the nurse's office for the student. Send along another student to assist if it appears necessary. When the illness is imaginary, malingerers are promptly returned. Never take a chance on an improper diagnosis yourself and keep the pupil in class. If the pupil is actually ill, you could find yourself on a limb facing a lawyer with a sharp saw.

I always had a standing policy that allowed all students who thought they were about to vomit to go directly outside or to the nurse's office immediately. It's wise not to require students to come to your desk and ask permission to leave the room in such circumstances. The reason should be obvious. You'll not find this policy being abused.

Children are prone to accidents. You'll be first on the scene of lots of accidents while teaching, so brush up on first aid. Most will be minor accidents. Take care of the problem and file a report later. The report is for your protection and should be done while events are still clear in your mind.

For more serious accidents send someone for the nurse while you keep the patient calm and control all agitated, curious youths who gather. Nurses have the facility to be at another school when needed, so take the precaution of also notifying the nearest administrator. The administrator will know whom to call for more immediate assistance and will be in a position to telephone for an ambulance should one be necessary. Having an administrator on the scene also gets you off the hook of responsibility.

Nurses take care of routine eye examinations, minor first aid, calling parents about ill students, and transporting injured students home with parent's permission. They keep health records and you should always check with the nurse about student health problems.

A SHOULDER TO CRY ON

Students have always needed someone to talk with about personal concerns. Teachers are available, but most pupils are reluctant to approach their teachers. Frequently they see the teacher as being the problem. Sometimes they're right.

Counselors are in schools to guide youngsters, to advise teachers in understanding each pupil's individual limitations or requirements, and to bridge the gap between home and school. Counselors have additional training in child psychology and counseling techniques beyond that required for regular teaching credentials. That is, they should have. A few are not fitted for the profession, as in any field.

Consult with the counselor about any student giving you frustrations. Chances are good that other teachers have the same concerns. Maybe the counselor can arrange a meeting with you, other teachers, parents, the counselor, and, sometimes, the child. The meeting could result in better student activity. At least, it will give you more insight into the problem.

The counselor might suggest transferring the student to another teacher. Let's face it. Students react differently with different teachers. Don't take it as a personal insult when a student makes no progress under your guidance. It's quite common. An understanding counselor will suggest what is best for the student. Isn't that what education is all about?

A good counselor won't be fooled by student accounts of what is bothering him or her. Once, a student I had had in a previous year was reassigned to me. The student told the counselor she wanted another teacher because I was the worst teacher in school. We agreed to transfer the student, but we transferred her to a different room than the one she had requested where all her friends were. Suddenly, mysteriously, I became the best teacher in school and she wanted to be back in my class.

Good counselors are an asset to a school, but, unfortunately, many counselors allow themselves to become the right arm of the principal. They become bogged down with routine matters such as student scheduling, school dances, parties, school yearbooks, and other trivia not altogether belonging under their jurisdiction. Some are given the unwelcome task of handling discipline cases, a duty not likely to gain the trust of students which is so necessary to counseling.

BOOKWORMS

Even low enrollment schools have a library of sorts. A corner in a room serves in some instances, but most schools set aside a room for library books. Larger schools have a librarian in charge. Get to know the librarian.

Librarians come in two classes. One type is so proud of the library that it is a joyous moment when approached for help. All stops are pulled out to be certain you are satisfied. A majority of librarians belong to this group. They assist in locating reference books and take hours to locate obscure materials whose existence is known only to them.

The other type is extremely jealous of the library and regards each book as a personal treasure not to be used by unclean hands. Book hoarding is common with this smaller group to keep precious books from slipping from their tight grasp. They regard students as an intrusion into their stronghold.

The first group is an asset to any learning situation. In their libraries, children thrive on learning library skills and enjoy checking out books. Even non-readers visit the library to look at pictures in magazines.

33

The second group turns children away from reading. Even youngsters who would rather curl up with a book than look at television frequently shy from the library. Let's hope your school is not saddled with a librarian of this caliber.

WHAT'S FOR LUNCH?

Some schools are phasing out cafeterias. Meals are brought from a central kitchen or students have to bring a lunch from home. Most schools still have a cafeteria where cooks doggedly attempt to prepare nutritious meals with an inadequate allowance from the business manager. You'll quickly learn if they are successful by noticing how many teachers bring a sack lunch to school.

A few schools have special meals and sometimes a separate dining room available for teachers. Most allow teachers to advance to the head of the lunch line, partly because teachers are adults and partly because teachers don't always have a duty-free lunchtime.

Expect to pay more than students. Don't expect a larger portion. Getting to know the cafeteria workers will give you someone to talk to as you buy lunch, but it won't increase the size of your meal. Cafeterias are not supposed to lose money, if possible.

Teachers seldom leave school grounds for lunch. There's not time enough even when restaurants are near. So, if you don't like what the school cafeteria offers, bring your own sack lunch. If you're lucky, the faculty has a microwave oven you can use.

GROUNDSMAN

Another fellow worker found around schools long before ecology became a household word is the gardener, or groundsman. The gardener's main object in life apparently is to mow the lawn outside a classroom whenever a teacher needs absolute silence. The day you have a sore throat and try to explain an intricate set of instructions to your class is the day the lawn is mowed outside your windows.

Gardeners also water lawns just prior to a teacher's taking a class outside to sit on the lawn to study a nature lesson. Some gardeners have the chore of squirting water on classroom windows to clean them. Once in a while you'll run across a gardener who closes them first.

Actually, it's amazing how gardeners manage to keep school grounds green and neat. Could you maintain shrubbery amidst hundreds of children doing impromptu pruning? Say a kind word to the gardener when you see him. He deserves it.

COMRADES-IN-ARMS

Then, of course, there are your fellow teachers. They are confined within classrooms so you'll not see some of them for days at a time. You'll get to know some of them better than others.

The teaching profession, like all others, has its share of mediocrity and fatuity. Avoid these persons and look for well-balanced individuals to share your teaching ideas and concerns. Teachers are anxious to give advice and you'll need it. Good teachers give good advice; poor teachers give poor advice. Poor advice makes the teaching road more precarious. Mingle with the better teachers and you'll upgrade your teaching skills.

This, then, makes up your comrades-in-arms. They are all in the battle to educate youngsters. Accept them as they are. You don't have to invite them home to dinner, but you do have to work with them. Some, I know, will become your friends for life.

4 CLASSROOM CONTROL

Discipline is a word bandied about in education classes by college professors who never define it in realistic terms. It's a word parents discuss at PTA meetings and it is the cause of frequent letters to newspapers. It's a word used constantly by politicians running for any office connected with education. Discipline is the elusive word in education that everyone professes to know, but no one understands.

AVOIDING THE ISSUE

There's an above-average chance when you're applying for a teaching position that some principal or personnel person will lean back in a chair and ask you how you handle discipline. Don't press the question and ask for a meaning of discipline. You'll only get a vague explanation, if any. They don't know. Impressions of discipline from persons not bottled inside a classroom with children vary greatly from a teacher's thoughts about discipline.

Don't expect an iron-clad explanation of discipline on these pages. The word is too nebulous, too intangible. Discipline has different meanings to different people. For some, it's students sitting rigidly in formal rows of desks listening to teacher's wisdom. Some think discipline means inflexible rules and regulations. Others define discipline as strict punishment for misdeeds. None are correct.

Teachers with thirty years on the firing line of public education still have problems with discipline—both in definition and in practice.

THE REAL WORD

What discipline really means, of course, is classroom control. Without control a teacher can throw in the sponge and seek employment in another line of work—as many do each year.

Discipline is classroom control. Easy to say, isn't it? Any college professor, parent, or school administrator can say it. Teachers say it. Doing is another matter.

TAKE CHARGE

Classroom control doesn't necessarily mean rigid control. Each student does not have to sit silently and obediently immobile in solemn, fixed rows of desks. Classroom control means the teacher is in complete charge and students are learning. There is no waste motion. At the teacher's direction students utilize maximum effort and achieve maximum success. I've visited classrooms where students walked around in seeming confusion, but observation revealed they were actually tending to tasks in an orderly manner under the teacher's control. There was no needless movement.

THE ANSWER

Maintaining effective classroom control is simple. You need only to have a learning program geared to each individual student's abilities and have it so stimulating that each student is completely wrapped up in the activities. Sounds great, huh?

Wouldn't teaching be pleasant if it was that easy? You can expect few days, if any, when you will have such a program. A typical classroom, say at the junior high level, might have students whose reading levels range from second to twelfth grade. There will be some with a short attention span. One or two will have physical difficulties serious enough to hinder their learning. Few will be curious enough to want to learn. All will have concerns not related to teacher's efforts.

Susie will be fretting about her boyfriend or girlfriend, Nancy daydreams in a fantasy world, Tim is upset because his mother is alcoholic, Joe is thinking of getting a job so he can buy a motorcycle, Betty hates school and all teachers, and so on.

In front of the group a teacher valiantly tries to whip up enthusiasm for the Battle of Hastings, English sentence structure, the Articles of Confederation or some other topic completely out of any student's sphere of reality. No teacher, no theory, can unite this class into a one-hundred-percent involvement with learning. No parent's storming into a PTA meeting and yelling about a lack of discipline will do the trick.

THE CHANGE

Even if, by some quirk, you have almost total involvement of a class in a project, there's no guarantee that the situation will be lasting. A class is a vibrant, restless personality in continual change. A new student enrolls, a disruptive student moves to a distant city, a holiday is about to begin, and the mood of the class is affected.

Nationwide, classroom behavior is shifting. Until recently the worst student behavior most schools expected was an occasional fistfight or a vulgar sketch scrawled in a textbook. Now some urban schools resort to guarded hallways to prevent knifings and vicious vandalism. Teachers are unprepared to alleviate the situation. In fact, sometimes the action or inaction of teachers and administrators fosters turmoil. Overlooking a tense condition makes it boil, not go away.

You could be assigned to a school where students fear to use the toilet facilities, or where, as in some schools, drinking fountain and toilet fixtures have been torn from their bases. In such schools, you face an uphill and probably losing battle with discipline. Your teaching lesson isn't going to register on a child fighting bladder control.

If you find yourself in such a position, take heart. Not all schools in the United States are like that. Most of them, because of community interest and/or strong administrative leadership, have only run-of-the-mill problems. If you find yourself teaching in an intolerable situation and you can't change the community, change to another community.

Perhaps, if teachers refuse to teach in schools where their lives are in danger, some action other than talking about discipline and blaming teachers for the lack of it will evolve.

HAVING AN EDGE

If you are faced with an unruly class, it would help you to have an edge. I remember one teacher who routinely tore thick telephone books in half when confronted with a new class. He wasn't a muscle man. He said there was a trick to it. Maybe learning the trick is the edge you need.

DISPLAY YOUR POWER

There's the story of another male teacher who took over a high school class in mid-year after the students had driven several other teachers from the room and from teaching. Recently discharged from the Marine Corps, the teacher arrived in full uniform complete with ribbons and marksmanship medals. Wordlessly, he removed his cap and placed it on his desk. Then he carefully draped his coat over his chair, removed his tie and finally his shirt. Still not saying a word, he turned his back to a silent, astonished class and rippled knotted arm and back muscles hardened by strenuous physical training. After a moment, he silently dressed. Straightening his tie to his satisfaction, he looked squarely at the class for the first time and inquired, "Any questions?" It is reported he had none of his predecessors' difficulties.

This method of control is not recommended for puny physical specimens or for females.

TOO MUCH POWER

Problems can certainly be lessened if you know the technique of pulverizing bricks with sharp, barehanded blows. Students will have something to talk about—and think about. Avoid bragging, but don't keep such information to yourself, either. I've worked with teachers who had won championships in swimming, female rodeo riding, track, and Golden Gloves without their students ever knowing of their accomplishments.

There was a teacher, a judo devotee, who never told his pupils of his expertness. One day a pupil, silently and playfully, slipped behind the teacher and poked him in the back. Startled and without thinking, the teacher automatically threw the pupil across a row of desks. The teacher was quite distressed. He was also lucky he wasn't sued.

THE STRAIGHT SHOOTER

Teachers have always had to contend with rowdy pupils. Some have faced the issue better than others.

Back in 1881 the San Francisco Chronicle reported about a teacher named Harry Flotoe who took over a one-room school in the Gold Rush town of Cranberry Gulch after its older pupils had already discouraged and disabled three teachers.

Understanding the nature of his pupils, the new teacher arrived wearing three revolvers and a Bowie knife with an eighteen-inch blade. Calmly he tacked a four-inch-square card to the wall. Then, walking across the room, he suddenly wheeled while drawing a revolver and fired six bullets into a spot the size of a silver dollar. Just as quickly, he threw the Bowie knife into the center of the card. Leaving it quivering as his room decoration, he conducted the class without mishap.

Harry's students came to love and respect him, but it is assumed you will seek to gain the love and respect of your pupils in a manner more suitable to modern times.

41

HELPFUL HINTS

So much for gloomy aspects of teaching. Thousands of teachers manage to maintain discipline without having serious problems. Let's remember that the primary purpose is to instruct, not emulate prison guards. With ordinary classes teachers should and do enjoy many rewarding moments and days. To ensure your share of them, a few tips follow. These ideas will not work with every student every time. They will work with some students some of the time.

KEEP 'EM BUSY

The first and most important tip is to keep your class actively doing something constructive. Make activities so interesting students don't realize learning is being accomplished. Stir interest by having them use their hands to build something, or by giving them choices of projects, or by having competitive activities. This takes careful planning, but you have to plan ahead anyway.

In history, for example, don't stick to a lecture-and-read program. Alternate with map drawing, debates, group reports, field trips to museums or local points of interest, play acting, and, especially in lower grades, building models of historic scenes or artifacts.

In English, underlining adjectives is important, but why not have students write descriptions of objects for other students to draw on the chalkboard? This exercise adds to an understanding of the use of adjectives and, at the same time, gives excellent practice in writing clear, easy-to-follow directions. The object being described should never be named to avoid preconceived ideas about its shape. Both you and the class will be amused at the weird interpretations of directions.

With high-interest activities three-fourths of your class will be too absorbed to cause problems. Most of the other fourth can be coerced or cajoled into taking part. Then you can concentrate on the few remaining class disrupters. Busy, challenged pupils tend to keep annoying troublemakers in line and ease your difficulties.

SET THE STANDARDS

Another tip is setting logical, enforceable rules and standards. Omit unnecessary standards and stick to your rules once you explain them to your pupils. Changing rules keeps students off balance and bewildered. Bewildered students compensate by being troublemakers.

Students always test teachers to see how far a rule can be bent. If your rules are not enforceable or are not consistent, you are the loser.

Set the tone of the class by your example. If students can't chew gum in class, you better not wander around chewing. If you want pupils to be on time, you had better be on time yourself and start lessons promptly so pupils will always know they'll miss instructions when they are tardy. If you want students to take school seriously, don't sit at your desk sipping coffee.

NIP IT IN THE BUD

One big help in maintaining classroom control is to stop troublemakers early. Let them know there is room for one boss and you are it. Be ready with swift, sure decisions to fit the occasion. Delayed, uncertain decisions are a sign of weakness students will recognize and take as a signal that they can put you on the defensive.

Never get into a verbal match with a pupil. You might possibly win an argument, but you'll always lose face. I remember one beginning teacher who was annoyed by a boy's playing with an object in class. When she asked why he was playing with the toy, the student replied, "Because I want to," and the verbal debate was on. The novice teacher escalated the problem by trying to snatch the object from the boy at his desk. The lad jumped up, and what had started as an inconsequential act terminated with the teacher chasing a laughing boy around the room as she tried to take away his toy. Her classroom discipline melted away to zero for the balance of the year.

Other and better ways to handle the situation would have been to ignore it, to demand the item be put away and stop all activity until it was out of sight, to talk to the student after class, to have the student come to the teacher's desk and leave the item, or to use peer pressure to bring him into the class activity. Any would be preferable to debating with the student. Incidentally, peer pressure is the most effective of the listed possibilities.

The problem began when the teacher asked a question. She should have made a firm, positive statement.

CALL HOME

One discipline help often ignored by teachers is calling parents. Let them know what's happening immediately. Don't wait until report cards are issued and surprise them. Often overlooked is the fact that parents have a genuine interest in their children and want them to succeed. They see their children's failures as reflections on themselves.

Telephone parents to discuss intolerable behavior at the first sign of a developing pattern. In many instances a simple telephone call corrects an incident and no problem evolves.

Not all parents respond favorably. Expect some to be highly indignant and verbally flay you when you imply that their offspring is less than perfect. I've found that patient listening until the parent runs down can sometimes bring the parent around to your side. Consider it, but if it appears to be a lost cause, think of the parent as part of the problem, not part of the treatment.

HOUSE CALLS

Making home visits is usually not advisable. Catching a parent in a cluttered house is not going to create better cooperation between home and school. Visit a home only if the parent insists and there's a logical reason.

I know of one teacher who was summoned to the home of the local crime boss after having given failing marks to the man's youngster. Arriving in trepidation, the teacher was relieved to be told to bear down on the youngster with full support from the father. The crime boss didn't want his child to be shirking an education. Most parents do care.

APPLY PRESSURE

Use your own students to help maintain discipline. Good students hate to be interrupted continually by a class clown. Let it be known that homework had to be assigned because the class clown delayed instruction within prescribed time limits. This technique works best when only a small minority of students cause trouble. Troublemaking is an attention-seeking device. When the device backfires, it is altered or it disappears.

Sometimes peer pressure is too strong. I remember one class clown's sporting a black eye after strolling behind the gym with fellow students and becoming a model student after the incident. He just hadn't realized he was annoying some of the better, and more athletic, students. They had impressed him with the importance of education in a more lasting manner than any teacher could.

THE OLD STANDBY

Old ways of discipline include having pupils write sentences over and over. Sometimes it's essays. As a beginner, I used these techniques. They weren't effective and I've never heard of any positive results with this method. Another old standby is having a pupil remain after school. This works sometimes under certain conditions.

Keeping students after school is useful if assignments are incomplete because of misbehavior and if the time is used to help students. It is not effective if students are merely required to sit and remain quiet.

Work with the students after school. Help youngsters to develop better attitudes. One former pupil of mine was so disruptive he was hated by the entire class. On his first report card his grades were the lowest possible in all areas. He remained after school on a daily basis to finish assignments and discuss behavior. Gradually he improved. At the end of the school year he had the highest grades earned both in academics and citizenship of all the one hundred eighty pupils I taught each day. More important, he earned the respect of many students and respectd himself.

Keeping students after school usually has less dramatic results. Usually it's more punishing for the teacher.

WARNING!

It is extremely unwise for a teacher to keep a student of the opposite sex after school at any grade level unless there are others present. The type of girl who exhibits poor behavior can also be the type of girl who spreads lies about teachers. When a student accuses a teacher of misconduct, strangely enough, it is the student's word that is accepted. Even after all charges are proven false, a cloud of suspicion lingers over the teacher's head and is passed on through the ranks of students and parents for years.

THE EVIL EYE

Classroom control is achieved better by calm, firm command. The old saying, "Count ten before you act," pays dividends in teaching. Making cool-headed decisions under emotional stress cannot be accomplished while screaming hysterically at an unruly youngster.

I found that doing no action works. For example, in an ordinary class with usually well-behaved youngsters there are occasions when a student will be mildly disruptive while instructions are being given. I stop talking and blandly look at the student without comment. Other class members wonder why the lesson has stopped and also look towards the offending pupil. Soon the student realizes something's wrong and looks up into dozens of pairs of eyes. Often this is enough to make the disruptive behavior stop. I continue the lesson without a word being said to the student.

Try it. It works. A long stare can be more effective than yelling. It also gives you time to think and you might avoid administering harsh penalties under the stress of the moment. Giving penalties too harsh for the offense will lose you the respect of your class, and students always work better with a teacher whom they respect.

BE FAIR

Students can tolerate a teacher who loads them with difficult assignments. They cannot tolerate a teacher whom they think is unfair.

If Joe is sent to the office for fighting with Susie, send Susie, too. If Tom is chastised for throwing a pencil, don't ignore it when Bill throws a pencil ten minutes later. If a test is announced, and students study long hours at home for it, don't say, "Oh, well, it wasn't important," and cancel the test.

Be consistent. Follow through with your rules. Whenever a change has to be made, discuss it with your class beforehand. Even primary children want a steady, consistent teacher who keeps them posted on what to expect.

KEEP IT PRIVATE

Whenever possible, talk to problem students out of earshot of their fellow classmates. Step outside with the student where you can talk quietly and still watch inside activities from the doorway.

Talking to a youngster away from the class does three things. First, it saves the student from the public embarrassment of being bawled out in front of friends and makes it easier to get to the root of the problem. Second, it permits a teacher to secure a commitment for better behavior without the student's being influenced by the presence of others. Third, it makes the balance of the class wonder about what's happening and this tends to curb their behavior.

GIVE 'EM A JOB

Classroom control includes doing routine matters with little or no confusion. Assign duties. Pupils like to help. Returning papers can be handled by students as soon as they learn to read names. Having a person assigned to return papers will free you for other things and it can be done without interrupting lessons.

If Sam knows he is to shut the windows five minutes prior to the end of school, he does it without fuss or disturbance.

Do rotate duties. Make it an honor if you so desire, but let the rowdy students have duties, too. I've found that some students change their attitudes about school when they feel important. They feel great when they can erase the chalkboard while other students have to sit at desks.

YOU'RE NOT GOD

The foregoing suggestions are not all the answers. A complete book on discipline could not cover every situation, but these ideas are based on experience, not theory. Some people not cooped up with children every day might not agree with them. However, I've seen them work. Other ideas will work as well.

A teacher is not God. Recognize that not all youngsters will respond to discipline. There are some who defy all rules of behavior. Sort them out early. These students should be sent to the vice-principal for action. Your job is to teach; your main responsibility is with the bulk of the youngsters. Why undergo emotional stress over the few who actually need professional help from psychologists? Remember, all children go to school. This includes all those who spend their adult years in prison or mental institutions.

It is not a reflection on your ability to acknowledge that you cannot control and inspire every youngster assigned to you.

5 ‖ COMMUNICATIONS

Teachers are in the communications business. Absorbing and passing on information is the bulk of a teacher's job. You'll spend most of your time communicating, not only with students, but also with parents, fellow teachers, other school personnel, and community leaders.

YOU GOTTA TALK

You might be shy and bashful, but you'll overcome it. Facing a roomful of students each day with eyes watching your every move and ears listening to every mispronounced word won't make you outgoing, but it will impel you to submerge your inner feelings. Children demand all your attention. You are forced to push away your self-consciousness.

You have to talk to children daily. You talk to them singly and by the roomful. It's good experience. Shy persons soon gain confidence and later find it's easier to talk before adult audiences because they're accustomed to standing before groups. In time, no matter how shy you are when you start teaching, you can talk before an auditorium filled with people. I don't say you'll enjoy it, just that you can do it.

PAPER, PAPER, PAPER

Lots of paper crosses a teacher's desk—class assignments, office memos, bulletins, newsletters, advertising from educational publishers, and notes from parents. Keep the circular file handy next to your desk. You might even need two waste baskets for all the paper you'll throw away.

Student assignments, corrected and given back to students, will also be tossed into waste baskets along with bulletins given pupils to be taken home to parents.

Some papers, because you think they'll have a future use, you'll save in cupboards where they will repose until the end of the school year when they, too, should be discarded. You'll find teachers who save every scrap of paper until their classrooms bulge. Don't bother. There's always more arriving.

SAVE 'EM

There is one group of papers you'll want to keep. You'll hang on to them for years. These papers are your touch with reality. They are the notes you receive from parents and children.

Treasure these notes. Protect them from harm. They tell it as it is. These notes will soar your spirits and bring you down to earth. They make you face yourself and your teaching ability. They will give you a glimpse of life.

Saved notes from parents and children have another, more selfish, use. Notes can be used as the basis of magazine articles or a book to help eke out your future inadequate retirement checks. It has happened. Why not to you?

I saved notes from parents and used some of them in a magazine article. The following samples were dredged out of a quarter century of memory. Unfortunately, the originals were destroyed in a fire.

A FEW GEMS

Dear teacher,

I will not sign a permission slip for Sally to go on a trip to the Museum of Man with her class. You stick to history. When she is old enough, I'll teach her about men.

****

Deer techer,

Why did you give Billy a f on his paper yesterday i red it and it was alrite if you gave him the low mark becuse of the greese marks that was my falt he let me read it an my hands was greesy.

****

Dear Teacher,

Thank you for lending Susie a quarter for lunch. I gave her money, but she forgot it. She is so forgetful all the time. Here is your quarter back.

Dear Teacher,

Enclosed is the quarter I forgot to put in the envelope yesterday.

****

Dear Teacher,

Can you assign my daughter to a study hall in the afternoon? She has glee club, typing, gym, and crafts in the morning and by noon she is too tired for the hard subjects.

****

Dear teacher,

I don't understand why you wrote that junior doesn't have good rapport in your class. He had all good grades on his last rapport card.

****

Dear Teacher,

Sue Ann wasn't feeling well this morning, but she did not want to miss any school. Could you call us if she doesn't feel better? We think she has the measles.

****

Dear Teacher,

What's the big idea of getting my son kicked out of school? He said you were nosing around in his locker where you had no right to be and caused all the trouble and had the whole school stand around in the playground while cops swarmed all over the place. Keep your nose out of other people's business. He was just going to wait until after school and then bring home the dynamite.

****

Dear teacher,

We can't understand why Donald is failing in arithmetic. We looked at his tests and he had a 25%, a 15%, a 35%, and a 10% and that adds up to 100%. He should be getting a good grade.

****

Dear Mr. Grass,

My daughter was quite upset yesterday because you wrote her name "Vickie" instead of "Vicki." She said you should have noticed she spelled it that way on the last paper she handed you.

Dear Mrs. Jones,

I am sorry your daughter was upset. I made the mistake of assuming that because your daughter had spelled her name "Vickie" all year she preferred that spelling.

Mr. Gauss

****

Dear Teacher,

Please excuse Janey for being late. Her horse broke loose and ran over to the neighbor's garden. We could have caught it, but our neighbor got excited and threw rocks at it and it tore down her clothesline. Then the cops came and took us around to find it. But they had to leave to see some crazy lady who saw a huge ghost in a white sheet rushing through her yard.

When we finally did get the horse, Janey had to walk it to cool it down, so that's why she didn't get to school until noon.

****

Your most delightful notes are ones students write you. Whether you think you are doing a great job or being a miserable failure, a quick perusal of these notes will bring things back into proper focus. The following is an example of a note that was both ego-strengthening and deflating.

Dear Teacher,

I think your a real nice english teacher. I had so much fun this year!

I permanently mounted the above note from an outstanding student and hung it in my study. It reminds me not to think learning is easy.

CALL RIGHT BACK

Much of your communication will be by telephone. Parents telephone teachers frequently and, as you are confined within a classroom and unable to answer the calls, you'll be notified by the office. Respond to each telephone call without delay when you have a free moment.

Respond no matter how distasteful you view the call. If it's important to a parent, it is important to you. Not calling back immediately is not only rude, but it makes you a less effective teacher. I've found that a personal talk over the telephone with a parent usually gains cooperation even when the parent is highly agitated. I've telephoned when parents have requested a personal interview at school and when parents have requested written progress reports for their children. Usually a telephone call solves the difficulty and it is faster than a conference within your classroom.

SPELL IT OUT

As a teacher, you'll write notes to parents. They can vary in form from long, involved reports to a brief word or two on a report card. Your image and your professional reputation ride home with those notes. Always double-check all your notes for grammar and spelling. The one sure way for a parent to remember you for years is to send out a note with a misspelled word. A teacher not spelling correctly is akin to a minister swearing like a battle-hardened soldier.

As a teacher, you will also circulate notes to other teachers or to the office. Carefully screen such messages for errors. Educators are primed to automatically notice written mistakes and, if you circulate notes containing errors, you will be inundated with returned notes having all mistakes neatly corrected in red ink. Proofread and save yourself embarrassment.

CHALK IT UP

You'll do lots of writing on a chalkboard. Much of it will be done while children watch, so proofread everything. Students take fiendish delight in exposing errors you make. Beat them to it and find your own mistakes.

Writing on a chalkboard differs from writing on paper in that you write larger letters and have to stand back from the board to read what you have written. Thus, it's possible for errors to happen.

You'll have occasions when you'll need to write on the chalkboard while illustrating a point to parents or teachers. Here, too, errors you make are always noticed although not necessarily brought to your attention.

At times, you'll conduct meetings before your fellow workers. Once, during such a meeting in front of teachers, principals, and the school district superintendent, I filled a chalkboard with sentences. In the rush of writing, I omitted a letter in a word. The mistake was noted and corrected by me during the course of the lecture, but my standing back from the board and proofreading the sentences could have eliminated both the error and my subsequent embarrassment.

PARENT CONFERENCES

Part of your communicating will be through parent conferences. It's common practice to substitute an individual conference with each parent in place of the traditional report card. Generally the school day is shortened for a few weeks to allow for the meetings.

Be prepared. Have samples of the child's work available to show the parent. Include both good and poor samples so parents can clearly understand both achievements and difficulties. Explain the year's program and what you expect the child to learn.

Many parents are uncomfortable in a school setting, so put them at ease. Be friendly, polite, and helpful. Encourage them to contribute to the conversation. It has a two-fold effect. The parents believe you are interested in their views and you gain knowledge about their children.

OPEN HOUSE

Often parent conferences take the form of an open house during which parents visit classrooms. These generally are held at night and you have to return to school for several hours. It makes for a long, tiring day.

At the junior and high school level, parents sometimes follow a shortened version of their youngster's schedule. If you have this type of open house, you can conduct the meetings by explaining in depth the yearly assignments and class expectations to the entire group. It's unwise to open such meetings to questions because a parent with a chip on the shoulder will take the opportunity to back you into a verbal corner. Field such attempts by asking for a personal conference after school. Many parents will not follow through with the conference, but, if they do, such a talk will be more beneficial.

Another type of open house allows parents to visit rooms at random for any length of time they desire during the evening. There's a basic fault with this. One parent might insist upon monopolizing the teacher's time to the exclusion of others. It promotes ill will if you ignore parents milling about your room, so politely, but firmly, break off conversation with a monopolizing parent and set a date when the parent can come to school and continue the discussion.

During open houses you should have samples of work done by students on display. Encourage parents to examine them. Parents who attend open house want to know what's being done. Others stay home.

WHOOPS!

Open houses occur early in the school year so, unless you teach one group of pupils a day, you might not be well acquainted with all your students. During one open house meeting, when I was teaching over two hundred junior high students a day, I had a long discussion with a parent about a boy named Terry. Part way through our talk it dawned on me that I was talking about the wrong student. The parent was talking about a daughter named Terry. After that I made certain I knew which child was being discussed before I carried on a conversation.

If it happens to you, quickly admit your error and discuss the correct child. It's quite easy to confuse names. Parents often have different last names than that of their children and many first names can be either a boy's name or a girl's name. Add to this the confused milling about and noise during an open house and it's possible for you not to grasp the proper name or to associate the name with a particular student.

THE PUBLIC

As a teacher you carry a responsibility you cannot ignore. The weight of our educational system rests upon your back. People listen to your opinions and your ideas. Yes, they do listen.

The public listens when you make a casual comment about school in the grocery store. People listen when you walk down the street and discuss student behavior with another teacher. They eavesdrop during your lively school-gripe session with your spouse while having breakfast in a coffee shop. So, accept a word to the wise. Be careful of what you say.

I know of educators who were in hot water and on the brink of lawsuits because of casual, light talking over dinner at a restaurant. They forgot that persons overhearing a conversation are likely to be related to or to be friends of the person being talked about.

Remember, too, that people like to gossip about schools, teachers, and anyone in authority. Your innocent conversation is grist for their gossip mill. You might be having a temporary problem with some pupil or with school administration. Listeners will latch onto this inside information and blow it into a full-scale matter that points out the reason schools are not doing a proper job of educating youngsters. Negative communication you don't need. Teaching is difficult enough.

6 ‖ EVALUATIONS

The idea of accountability has been gaining force in education for years. Factory products can be machined and stamped out with few imperfections, so why not school children? Why not hold the teacher accountable for the end product? If Johnny can't read, hold his teacher responsible and overlook the other thirty-six children in the class who did learn to read.

STILL BULL

Several years ago California passed a law to assess teachers' effectiveness. Named for its chief legislative proponent, the Stull Bill—quickly renamed the Still Bull by educators—created widespread confusion because of its various interpretations. One aspect of the bill was to gauge a teacher's worth by his or her ability to have students reach certain goals, so throughout California administrators required school faculties to hold numerous meetings to write goals and objectives.

This was fine. Teachers need to know their goals. However, as with many things thrust upon employees, the idea was poorly received and carried out. Ignored was the fact that every teacher was already striving for certain objectives. Otherwise, teaching has little meaning.

Administrators forced teachers to submit detailed outlines of their courses and made them test and retest their students to see if expectancies were being achieved.

Time badly needed for lesson preparation and paper checking was sacrificed to write goals and fill out detailed progress charts to satisfy principals' whims. Many teachers gave pretests and tests to prove to administrators how great they were. Since teachers made their own tests, some results were highly spectacular. They taught for the tests with a resulting loss of spontaneous creativity. The final result remained unchanged. Some children read well; some don't.

UNDER CLOSE SCRUTINY

Actually, teachers have always been held accountable for their actions many times over. A factory employee is held accountable by an immediate superior. Teachers are not so lucky. They are being evaluated not only by an immediate superior, but by fellow educators, the general public, and all children.

Students continuously scrutinize teachers for hours each day and note every detail of mismatched clothing, odd mannerisms, or unusual speech accents. These are filed away in memory to be recalled later in discussions with parents and peers. The more outrageous an action, the more memorable it becomes.

One memory cherished by a group of former high school students dates back to World War II when elastic was inferior and undependable. The elastic holding an unfortunate female teacher's panties failed to function and the unmentionable garment dropped to her ankles during a class lecture. Outwardly unruffled, she kicked the perverse article under her desk without pausing in her talk. News of her shame and bravery flashed throughout the student body by way of its mysterious communication system even before her class was dismissed. Her former students still give her a superior rating for calmness under stress.

DOUBLE TROUBLE

As a teacher you always will be evaluated by the general public. Your dress, actions, and speech will be noted and remarked upon whether you shop in a store or visit the neighborhood bar. Things that go unnoticed when done by others take on a new light when done by a teacher. Maybe it's

62

a throwback to their childhood spent in school, but it delights people to discover that teachers are not perfect. Perhaps it makes them feel superior for a moment.

Newspapers might ignore a report of a woman arrested for drunken driving, but if she is a teacher, the arrest rates newspaper space complete with headlines mentioning her occupation. Few other occupations rate such notice.

A plumber arrested for the same offense could be in for some good-natured joshing from friends. A teacher faces more severe punishment.

State credentials commissions revoke teaching credentials of persons convicted of a felony. Thus, a teacher, unlike a plumber, can be tried and punished twice for the same offense. A teacher convicted of drunken driving would not only possibly serve time behind bars, but such a teacher could also lose a career and livelihood. There is good reason for removing teachers from classrooms after being convicted of crimes, but whether you agree they should be removed or not, it is necessary for you to be aware of the consequences of your actions. People expect teachers to display the same characteristics they imagine nuns and monks to have.

STOPPED BEFORE STARTING

I know of two persons who faced the double jeopardy obstacle before they could start teaching. One, a recent high school graduate, celebrated graduation by drinking a few beers with friends before he left for college. Driving erratically three blocks to his home, he was stopped by a policeman and arrested for drunken driving. He was released with a light fine, but he was ineligible to begin a college program leading to an education degree.

The other person was overjoyed to land a hard-to-get contract to teach high school woodworking. His enthusiasm was short-lived. As a craftsman who spent days at home creating furniture in his garage, he was viewed with suspicion by a neighbor whose three-year-old daughter often played with the craftsman's daughter. One day the neighbor's daughter arrived home without her shirt and with a dab of paint on her stomach. The mother had the prospective teacher arrested for child molestation. He was completely vindicated and his arrest record was removed from the books by the police because the charges were proven to be so totally false and malicious.

Yet, the state credentials commission held a hearing and, although the mother kept changing her story and the craftsman had numerous witnesses attesting to his virtuous life, the teaching credential was denied. Without it, of course, he could not teach.

PROFESSIONAL ATTACKERS

There are people who see the worst in any situation. They have some quirk that makes them think they are *right* and you are wrong. Remember, not everyone shares your view of life. What you regard as a simple classroom exercise can be twisted into your nightmare when others evaluate your efforts through their prejudices.

One teacher who presented a recommended, not required, reading list in an English class found himself suddenly the object of abusive telephone calls, letters to the newspaper, meetings of outraged parents, and chastisement by the school board.

This teacher struggled for years under an attack fostered by stormy letters to the editor in the local newspaper. He never did understand why the book list generated so much trouble.

Years after the incident a retired executive of a large corporation casually mentioned how he had "gotten" a teacher who had tried to "brainwash" his daughter. To give credence to his statement, he showed yellowed copies of letters he had written to newspapers protesting the teacher's actions. On each letter he used a different fictitious name and letterhead. The bewildered English teacher and the public were never aware that the whole campaign had been the work of one person.

The chance of your being on the receiving end of such actions is slim. Most teachers complete their entire career without incident. Events cited in this book are merely to alert you to possibilities so you won't place yourself in an undesirable position. A person knowing the road is rocky is less likely to stumble.

THE BACKUP

When you are on the receiving end of a parent's wrath, an administrator might back you—possibly into a corner, that is. Administrators don't like waves. Waves tip over boats and dump administrators into hot water. Naturally, they all worry about keeping Number One afloat.

Some teachers keep detailed notes of worrisome events they think will cause them trouble. I once thought they were paranoid. Now I'm not so sure. Having detailed records can be a safety net if things blow up in your face.

One knowledgeable teacher of remedial-type pupils always kept records of unusual student behavior and almost hit paydirt. Observing a pair of students acting in a manner not condoned in school settings, he informed them their actions didn't tie in with their present class assignment. The girl, enraged, swore at the teacher and vowed she would have him fired.

The next afternoon the teacher was pulled into a quick conference with two outraged, moralistic parents, several indignant administrators and a very innocent and chaste example of childhood. The group listened as the girl told her story in Puritan-like tones. Her outlandish tale was followed by the administrators demanding that the teacher apologize to the girl and by the two agitated, screeching parents threatening lawsuits in an intense, heated outpouring of anger.

Throughout the bedlam the teacher remained calm and quiet. He closed his ears to threats of dismissal and lawsuits and dreamed of basking in the Hawaiian sun with money gained in countersuits. He knew he had witnesses and written evidence on his side.

His dream suddenly vanished. The young pillar of virtue didn't have the staying power of her parents. Tired of the loud discussion and hard chair she sat on, she stood up and from her pristine lips spouted, "I'm tired of all this G-- d--- s---. Let's get the f--- out of here!"

The girl was dragged from the room by parents yelling four-letter obscenities at her for ruining a sure-fire lawsuit, the administrators beat a hasty, red-faced retreat, and the teacher was left without the Hawaiian trip.

FORMAL EVALUATIONS

By now you might have second thoughts about wanting to teach. Remember, experiences mentioned in this book are rare examples and are told to keep you on your toes and to remind you of the public's informal evaluations.

Formal evaluations will concern you more directly. Principals are supposed to watch your methods and determine how effective you are in the classroom. When and how they enter your room to observe you in action varies from school to school depending on district policy and a principal's inclination.

Generally, principals must complete a written evaluation of your work. Some districts use a checklist on which the principal places checkmarks in appropriate boxes. Many districts require written paragraphs about you and others use a combination of checklists and written comments.

Some districts rate a teacher every few years; others rate teachers frequently. As a beginning teacher you can expect to be evaluated more often than an oldtimer. Don't worry about it. Assuming you do an adequate job, you'll be fairly judged.

Keep in mind that the principal doesn't like to step into your classroom and judge your methods any more than you look forward to it.

THE WATCHFUL EYE

Some principals walk into rooms unannounced; some make appointments. If possible, set a certain time for the principal to visit your room so you can be prepared. This method actually allows the principal to view your teaching techniques better. Unannounced visits tend to happen just as you are about to show films or engage in boring, routine lessons.

Always ask for a conference after a principal has visited your room. Go over your strong and weak points and seek advice on how to improve. You don't often get such a chance to learn how others view your actions. Some principals automatically schedule a conference while others tend to keep you in the dark. You be the one to insist on a conference if the principal doesn't. Delay it, and you'll sit around worrying and wondering.

DON'T FRET ABOUT EVALUATIONS

Many teachers become flustered when visitors enter the classroom. You need not worry.

One teacher well remembers her first formal evaluation. An elderly administrator waddled into her room unannounced and plumped down, pad and pencil in hand, in an empty desk at the back of the room. When the lesson began the teacher was quite confident, but, as the hour dragged on and the figure hunched over an evaluation pad did not glance up to give any hint of approval or disapproval, confidence oozed away. The teacher threw herself into the lesson with more and more fervor and produced a response in the children never before achieved. Still there was no acknowledgement from the evaluator. It wasn't until the dismissal bell rang and the evaluator's head roused with a start that the moment of truth dawned. The evaluator had fallen asleep. But the children did receive exceptional teaching and that's the reason for evaluations, anyway.

VISITS FROM THE BRASS

Occasionally, high brass might wander into your room. The school district superintendent and the superintendent of instruction, if your district has one, like to report back to the school board about how well they keep tabs on the district teaching staff. Usually the visit is short and is guided by the principal who steers them into rooms where good teaching occurs. Your principal is no fool. Good reports at the district level reflect on the principal.

One newly-hired teacher was teaching English without textbooks because he thought the ones issued were lacking basic instruction. Suddenly the assistant superintendent of the district wandered into his room unannounced. The teacher was dismayed but plunged ahead with the lesson as though it was the most important thing in the world. The administrator stood in the back of the room watching every move while the teacher continued to illustrate his grammar lesson on the chalkboard.

At the end of the hour the administrator was still in the back of the room and the teacher, knowing it was the policy of the assistant superintendent to make only token appearances in classrooms, was a bundle of nerves.

Then, leaving the room, the administrator quelled the teacher's fears. He shook his hand, saying, "I didn't intend to stay so long, but I became so absorbed in what I was learning I couldn't leave. I learned something I never understood before."

Administrators are humans. Some of them went into administration because they were failures in teaching. They don't know it all. Don't let it shake you up when one of them

68

enters your room. Just hope it's at a good time and not bedlam when it happens.

NO PERFECT ANSWER

All working people are evaluated by someone. Expect it as a teacher. Don't expect a perfect way to be evaluated. Controversy has been raging for years over evaluations and no answer has been found. School districts routinely change evaluation forms hoping to improve. They don't. They just follow cycles.

At the end of this chapter is a satire I wrote in 1962 to poke fun at evaluation forms and show the inaccuracy of one's judgments of others. To illustrate that evaluations are still much on people's minds, this satire has been in continuous publication in books and magazines in the United States and England since it first appeared in Phi Delta Kappan, an education magazine.

STRANGERS DROP IN

Occasionally a stranger will wander into your class. In most districts it is a policy for visitors to check in at the school office. Some people do; some don't.

I usually handled these drop-in visits by continuing with the lesson until it was convenient to walk to the door where the visitor usually stood. Then I introduced myself and asked the nature of the visit.

If the visitor was a college student or someone sent to observe teaching methods, I sat the person down and provided a copy of the textbook or whatever papers we were studying. The same procedure was followed for a student's parents.

Frequently, I changed lessons slightly to fit the circumstance. For parent visits, I altered plans so I could call upon the son or daughter to answer questions or do some assignment to demonstrate prowess. In a case where someone wanted to observe teaching methods, I varied lessons within the hour to reveal as many techniques as possible.

I remember one irate parent who sat in my room for over an hour to get proof of my ineffective teaching. His son had been transferred into my room after receiving a "B" on his report card. I called them as I saw them. His son received "D" from me.

During the man's stay I called upon his son as frequently as possible to demonstrate his ability. This meant changing my program so I had reason to call on different members of the class. At the end of the hour the man was convinced. His son was not another Einstein. I showed the father my grade book to cinch the fact that the "D" grade was not only the best he had done, but probably a gift as well.

You'll run into this while teaching. Some teachers hate to admit failure and try to avoid parent conflicts by boosting student grades. It makes it difficult for the rest of the teachers, especially those who follow.

YOUR CHANCE

This, then, is your fate. You'll always be evaluated. You can't escape it. Formal evaluations are the easy ones. You can prime yourself for them. The others are more difficult and harder to fight if you feel unfairly judged.

However, you do your share of evaluating, too. Every child in your classes is evaluated by you every day. Try to remember how you feel about unfair evaluations when you mark papers and report cards. This does not mean you should raise grades. Just be consistent and grade fairly. If too many students are receiving low grades, review your methods and correct your own faults. Gear the lessons to the ability of your class.

Do keep a running account of all grades in a grade book and talk to students who are lagging behind the rest of the class. This eliminates report card shock and shows students you are interested in their progress and expect to see improvement.

Teacher Evaluation

Teacher: Socrates

A. Personal Qualifications

	Rating (high to low)					Comments
	1	2	3	4	5	
1. Personal appearance	☐	☐	☐	☐	☑	*Dresses in an old sheet draped about his body*
2. Self-confidence	☐	☐	☐	☐	☑	*Not sure of himself—always asking questions*
3. Use of English	☐	☐	☐	☑	☐	*Speaks with a heavy Greek accent*
4. Adaptability	☐	☐	☐	☐	☑	*Prone to suicide by poison when under duress*

B. Class Management

	1	2	3	4	5	
1. Organization	☐	☐	☐	☐	☑	*Does not keep a seating chart*
2. Room appearance	☐	☐	☐	☑	☐	*Does not have eye-catching bulletin boards*
3. Utilization of supplies	☑	☐	☐	☐	☐	*Does not use supplies*

C. Teacher-Pupil Relationships

	1	2	3	4	5	
1. Tact and consideration	☐	☐	☐	☐	☑	*Places student in embarrassing situation by asking questions*
2. Attitude of class	☐	☑	☐	☐	☐	*Class is friendly*

D. Techniques of Teaching

	1	2	3	4	5	
1. Daily preparation	☐	☐	☐	☐	☑	*Does not keep daily lesson plans*
2. Attention to course of study	☐	☐	☑	☐	☐	*Quite flexible—allows students to wander to different topics*
3. Knowledge of subject matter	☐	☐	☐	☐	☑	*Does not know material—has to question pupils to gain knowledge*

E. Professional Attitude

	1	2	3	4	5	
1. Professional ethics	☐	☐	☐	☐	☑	*Does not belong to professional association or PTA*
2. In-service training	☐	☐	☐	☐	☑	*Complete failure here—has not even bothered to attend college*
3. Parent relationships	☐	☐	☐	☐	☑	*Needs to improve in this area— parents are trying to get rid of him*

Recommendation: DOES NOT HAVE A PLACE IN EDUCATION—SHOULD NOT BE REHIRE

"Evaluation of Socrates as a Teacher," by John Gauss, Phi Delta Kappan, January 1962.

7 ‖ PAPERS AND PATIENCE

Correcting student-written papers is a dull, eye-tiring chore all teachers endure. Time-consuming and discouraging, it's a main part of the job, but you knew that before you entered college to seek a teaching credential.

It's hoped this chapter will provide a few hints to minimize paper grading so your evenings can be your own.

THE SUBJECT MATTERS

The best way to lessen eyestrain is to teach a subject requiring little reading of student papers. This is generally possible only if you prepared yourself with the right background and only if one of the scarce positions is available. As you might imagine, there are few openings.

Shop, art, band, cooking, and physical education are among those classes usually taught with minimum written assignments. Occasionally, science teachers can arrange assignments requiring little written work, but, as a rule, most science teachers are as deluged with student papers as other teachers. In typing classes, students deplete reams of paper, but easy-to-check lessons can necessitate slight teacher effort.

Naturally, each of the mentioned subjects comes with its own built-in problems, and, to many teachers, traditional subjects complete with paperwork burdens are preferable. For instance, band teachers, besieged by a constant din from poorly-played band instruments, might crave ears of steel while shop teachers cringe repeatedly while watching inept

73

students casually manipulate sharp chisels amid crowded work areas. Shop teachers consider first aid kits a must. However, they do benefit from fewer paper-grading sessions.

All classes require occasional light paper grading from time to time, but teaching a subject such as art or sewing where a quick glance can catch errors without undue eyestrain certainly lessens the onerous chore.

Teachers shy from teaching English with its daily piles of papers to check. Plan on evenings cuddled with students' papers instead of a friend if you teach English. History and mathematics classes also stack papers on a teacher's desk, but to a lesser extent, and teaching these subjects will allow you more free evenings than those enjoyed by English teachers.

GRADE LEVELS

Picking the right grade level also eases paperwork chores. A primary teacher watching pupils slowly form each letter as they write will have less to read than a high school history teacher who unwisely has one hundred fifty students handing in lengthy written reports on the same day.

As children mature they write more, make more mistakes for you to find, and develop more outlandish handwritings. All this makes paper-checking tougher. Children also do less picture painting as they progress through school. So, if you work with lower elementary grade students, you won't necessarily have an easier time in the classroom, but you will have an easier time handling papers.

LAUGH IT OFF

Secondary school teachers, although correcting more written papers and less artwork than primary teachers, do have one advantage. They get more occasional chuckles reading student errors. It relieves tedium while reading dozens of identical papers containing identical information and identical errors.

Treasure these written gems whenever a misspelled word or mixed-up sentence structure produces a smile. Maybe you can publish them along with those notes from home you are collecting.

The following bits of misinformation lightened a few of my dull paper-checking sessions.

> I enjoyed reading the Rapes of Wrath because it was right down my alley.

> The President heads the Executioner branch of government.

> After it was captured again she visited her bare at the zoo.

> The Middle Ages are called the Dark Ages because people don't like to be called Middle Aged.

> The dune buggy crawled over the sandy dessert.

> My life is impotent to me.

PROMPT RETURN

Make it a policy to check and return student papers immediately. Students not only learn faster by seeing their mistakes soon after making them, but you aren't overwhelmed by stacks of papers accumulating on your desk.

If possible, check papers in class and have them back in pupils' hands the same day. It's not as difficult as you might believe and can be done several ways.

Schedule assignments to allow you to correct essays while your class quietly does arithmetic or reads. Give short assignments so they can be read and checked quickly. Students learn as much writing a paragraph as they do writing a page. Short written assignments are also more easily rewritten by students whenever you require them to correct their mistakes.

Use answer columns for arithmetic and history tests. Having students write answers in a column along the side of their papers saves your time and eases eyestrain. With the use of answer columns, I've often been able to begin checking papers as soon as the first student finished a test and had all grades recorded and tests returned shortly after the last student finished. Naturally, all students had other tasks to do after completing their tests. Having students sit idle is not going to permit you to accomplish your own tasks because they'll kill time in a manner not soothing to your nervous system.

Incidentally, if you teach more than one class and intend to use the same tests, don't return quiz papers until the last student has taken the test. The reason is obvious.

The use of answer columns in arithmetic should not omit the necessity of having students show all their work in a neat, logical order. It just makes it easier for you to pinpoint their mistakes.

Many subjects lend themselves to an answer column for short answers. Science or history teachers occasionally give tests using sentences with one word missing. Why not require that the word be placed in an answer column as well as being placed within the sentence? You'll be amazed at the ease of checking answers.

HONOR SYSTEM

Most students can check their own papers. Give out the correct responses and let them find their mistakes. An alternative is to have students exchange papers and correct someone else's so they can learn to spot errors. This technique works well for routine, practice-type papers. Spot-check papers yourself if grades are to be recorded. Students are not as tuned to finding errors as you are.

Spelling tests can easily be graded by students. Simply say the correct spellings as students check their own or another person's paper. There is always temptation to cheat or "help a

76

friend," so you should check enough of the tests yourself to determine if results are accurate.

Occasionally, reliable students will want to check papers for you. Let them if it's an easy-to-check assignment. Again, spot-check the papers before you record grades.

SPREAD OUT

Spread out assignments. Don't fall into the trap of making Friday test day. Keep papers dribbling in all week so you can pace yourself. You set up all assignments. It's your own fault if you are swamped with papers.

Throw in a few easy-to-grade assignments when you need to catch your breath. Oral reports and graph-making keep students gainfully occupied and are easy to check.

If you teach the same subject several times a day in a secondary school, plan your lessons so each class is not a repeat performance. While one class is doing research for future extensive reports, you can be grading reports from another class.

CHALK IT UP

Make good use of the chalkboard. Let pupils write on it frequently. They enjoy doing so. With English classes, for example, you might have them locate adjectives in sentences on the board or have them write their own sentences.

Let them use the chalkboard to figure arithmetic problems or draw the parts of a flower in chalk. Make a sport of it by having team competitions. You eliminate papers to check and it stirs interest in otherwise dull activities.

Write a paragraph on the chalkboard yourself and let various members of the class locate your deliberate errors or improve your paragraph. Encourage class members to orally name or chalk in missing items from a diagram or a list you place on the chalkboard. Learning is still accomplished and your evenings are your own.

GETTING CARRIED AWAY

In your search for ways to eliminate paper checking, don't let enthusiasm overcome prudent judgment. Once, while passing near a school, I noticed a youngster standing in the middle of a street a block away. When asked what he was doing, he stated that his science teacher was illustrating the magnitude of our solar system and had students assume the positions of various planets. This youngster was Pluto.

You can easily guess whose neck would have been on the line if the student had been injured by an automobile. The teacher would have been on safer ground by asking the class to draw the solar system on paper.

KEEP RECORDS

Record all grades from all papers. It takes time, but it's worth every minute because general achievement trends soon become apparent. Also, students will swear they completed all assignments, but a look at the grade book can convince even stubborn doubters. Blank spots show up like red flags.

I remember one parent's expressing surprise at seeing all the blank spots after her son's name in the grade book. She had supervised his homework every night and knew he had finished it. Upon confronting her son, she discovered he had kept all papers and stuffed them under his bed. Why, I never knew.

Keeping an up-to-date grade book can help back up statements to parents and simplify completing report cards. The more grades, the easier it is to evaluate progress. Incidentally, I used numbers instead of letter grades in my grade book—5 for A, 4 for B, etc.. Faster to add up and average, you know.

REPORT CARDS

Educators don't like report cards. There is no perfect answer to evaluating student progress and report cards fall short of doing an adequate job. At best, they give parents and students a hazy idea of how a student does as compared to whatever standards a teacher sets. A letter grade in one teacher's class actually has little in common with a grade given by another teacher.

Parents lulled into a false idea of their offspring's progress are jolted when their child is transferred to a different teacher who has different standards. Expect to be questioned by parents if your grading standards are higher than those of a previous teacher. Somehow, parents don't question it if their youngster suddenly receives better marks, but they blame teachers for lower marks. Perhaps this is why grading standards have been lowered in recent years.

THE IMPOSSIBLE QUEST

Report cards are here to stay. Chances are you'll be on one or more committees during your teaching career trying to rough out a perfect report card. Some districts change the forms every few years seeking the ultimate answer. It never works. It's impossible to register any child's failings and achievements in short, formalized announcements. However, parents do want to know their children's progress and a report card is the quickest, easiest way to inform parents en masse.

THE CARD'S INFLUENCE

Although a report card is not always a reliable gauge of a pupil's progress, it can certainly affect attitudes toward school. I remember a boy who enjoyed going to kindergarten with his friends, but after promotion to first grade, he hated school. Every morning his parents had to shove him out the door and force him to leave for the schoolhouse. They were perplexed about their son's sudden change.

The mystery was solved after the boy received his first report card and rushed into his house after school yelling, "She likes me. The teacher likes me!" His first grade teacher always offered a stern facade at the beginning of each school year to ensure a "no-nonsense" approach to learning. The boy misunderstood it to mean she didn't like him. A good report card with a brief comment stating how pleasant it was to have the boy in her class cleared the air. The next morning the boy dashed to school early and his enthusiasm remained even throughout his college years where he graduated with honors.

Take time to offer brief, constructive comments on report cards. It's not easy, but you might be molding some person's lifelong attitude towards learning.

THE DIPLOMAT

Writing positive comments on some children's report cards can stretch your imagination to the limit. How do you write that the apple-of-someone's-eye is a class clown and operating with a short circuit to the brain?

Be diplomatic. Teachers rarely inform parents what they really think about problem children. It's much easier to write chatty comments about a child who is a teacher's dream; not a teacher's nightmare. Telling parents that their child is batting zero and classmates cheer when the youngster's name appears on the absence list is not good public relations. Still, I've often found that it's possible to be blunt and also write about a child in such a way that no feelings are offended. Just choose your words carefully.

Accept the fact that several of the children you teach will spend time in prison or mental institutions during their lifetimes. Many of these same people do poorly in school and if you ignore writing about any scholastic or behavioral problems they reveal, you're sidestepping your responsibilities. Parents depend upon teachers to alert them to potential problems, although they undoubtedly won't thank you for it and might shove all the blame on your shoulders.

The tongue-in-cheek guideline accompanying this chapter is more accurate than you might believe. Successful teachers seldom write exactly what they consider the truth. They disguise facts with verbiage because they want to devote lives to teaching, not making lawyers happy.

TEACHER-TO-PARENT REPORTS GUIDELINE

WHEN YOU MEAN: Your Child...	THEN WRITE: Your Child...
is really weird	a. exhibits exceptional behavior b. is maturing slowly
has me batting my head against the wall	a. has difficulty adjusting to our requirements b. adapts poorly to discipline c. might establish better rapport with another teacher
has other pupils wanting to bat your offspring's head against the wall	a. does not make friends easily b. has undeveloped peer relationships c. has poor interaction with others
is learning as much as a grapefruit	a. needs to concentrate on assigned lessons b. is not achieving at the required level
rates somewhere below a rock mentally	a. is progressing at his/her utmost ability b. is proceeding at expected levels of achievement
has the behavior of a chimpanzee	a. does not adjust well to social situations b. is the focal point of the class
acts like a bitch in heat	a. shows remarkable maturity b. makes friends quite easily

8 | RESPONSIBILITY AND LAWSUITS

Teachers often unknowingly perch on the brink of lawsuits and the fact that few teachers are sued is more pure luck than an absence of reasons. Browse through a copy of an education code or an education lawbook and you'll find laws protecting teachers. Read between the lines and you'll find the protection as useful as a quarter inch of ice on an ice-skating pond.

NEGLIGENCE

Frequently court cases involving teachers are based on a teacher's negligence, but teachers can also be named in lawsuits when school districts are sued.

For instance, suppose a pupil is injured using defective playground equipment while under your supervision. Whose fault is it—yours or the school district's? Parents and lawyers are quick to list all possible responsible parties in lawsuits so you could possibly share the accusation, especially if you knew and failed to report that the equipment needed repair.

HEALTH AND WELFARE

Most likely, if you find yourself in court, it will be based on something injurious to the health or welfare of students. Your being an inept teacher is an administrative matter handled within your school district and is not likely to become a court case unless you object to an unfavorable decision and insist on having a court hearing. Remember, you can be fired for being a lousy teacher; you can be sued for causing harm or anguish to students.

As a teacher you are always responsible for any children assigned to your control or any children within your area of vision or hearing at school. Students leaving your room to use the restroom, even if you are not aware of their leaving, are still your responsibility. Should a student be injured enroute or while in the restroom, you could be sued by an irate parent.

BE PRUDENT

If you do find yourself in court, the judge is likely to base part of his decision on whether you used good judgment and acted in a prudent manner. Teachers doing all that any responsible person would have done *having the teacher's experience and knowledge of children* stand an excellent chance of receiving a favorable decision. However, if it is proved you acted unwisely, the case could be your exit from teaching.

You'll sleep better nights by avoiding courtroom-bound circumstances entirely, but that's nearly impossible. Luck will keep you out of court.

EMERGENCY LEAVE

Suppose your well-behaved class is quietly reading. There have been no problems and you expect none. Suddenly the meal you ate last evening at Ptomaine Palace seizes your stomach in severe cramps. An immediate rush to the nearest restroom is imperative lest your clothing becomes embarrassingly soiled.

You are aware of your responsibility and know the class has to be under a reasonable degree of supervision at all times. Yet, you must leave. What would you do?

Or suppose a parent or teacher beckons you to the door and wants to talk to you confidentially in the corridor away from children's ears. Should you step out of the room?

In the first example, you have little choice but to leave, of course. A judge might consider that reasonable. However, if your class is left unsupervised, a judge could be less understanding.

You actually have several options besides the obvious, undesirable one of remaining. One possibility is pausing at the door of an adjoining room and asking that teacher to watch your class for a moment. Most neighboring teachers can easily oversee your class by either standing in a position enabling them to look into both rooms or by occasionally walking into your room.

Second, yours might be one of the few schools having a telephone or intercom within classrooms. If so, notify the office to send someone immediately. Wait until assistance arrives, if possible. If not, you are at least covered.

Third, send a reliable student to request help from the office. A principal's duties include assisting teachers in time of stress, so the principal should either assume the duty or assign a person to watch your class.

Your fourth alternative is to place your most responsible student in charge and pray a lot.

In the case where someone beckons you to the doorway, you have two choices. Either ask the person for a later conference or position yourself outside your doorway so you have a clear view of the interior and talk in low tones. Be prepared to step back into the classroom if necessary.

Courts have ruled that reasonable care had been exercised and a teacher was not negligent if another teacher had observed the class periodically. Thus, a court knows there are emergencies and it is not always possible for a class to be under constant scrutiny. You, however, must prove you were not negligent during the emergency. Leaving the room to make a personal telephone call would possibly not be considered a prudent act.

WRAPPED UP IN YOUR WORK

Suppose you are busily checking papers at your desk in front of the classroom. You are completely absorbed in your work and the pupils are quietly reading or figuring arithmetic problems. Nothing can go wrong. Are you in danger of being sued? Surprisingly, the answer is yes.

It doesn't pay to become complacent because children are sneaky and can be expected to do the unexpected. One court ruled the teacher negligent after a student threw a metal object which hit another student in the eye during classtime. Bits of metal previously being tossed about the room had been unobserved by the teacher. The court noted that the teacher should have seen and stopped the action.

Position your desk to obtain maximum observation of your pupils and don't become so engrossed in your desk work that you fail to glance at the class from time to time. It's your neck you're protecting, so nip unwanted pupil behavior before it sends you to court.

PUNISHING YOURSELF

Punishing a pupil is punishing yourself. This is true no matter how justified the act. The pupil's anguish won't be any greater than yours. Conscientious teachers lie awake nights wondering whether their methods were correct and worrying about consequences, especially if physical punishment was used. Physical punishment, such as spanking, might not be harmful to a child, but it can be disastrous to your career.

If you do think spanking is the only answer, turn your problem over to an administrator. Your principal is paid to solve problems. Also, if spanking appears to be the only actual solution, an administrator can do it without being accused of malice as you might be. Incidentally, spanking is frowned upon by many people and most school districts have a policy governing spankings. Many districts forbid them. It's doubtful if they're effective in deterring irksome behavior.

Keeping pupils after school is a common punishment. Generally, it produces negative results and lines you up for a lawsuit if it can be shown you placed a child in jeopardy. For instance, suppose your actions cause a child to miss a bus and the child walks home in the worst blizzard in history. Or suppose the child arrives home after dark and suffers harm or discomfort. Some parents would be displeased enough to sue you.

RIDING INTO TROUBLE

A secondary school teacher of problem children suffered the discomfort and expense of a lawsuit because one of his students rode a moped to school and was allowed to park it in the room and ride it home after school. The student rode home and then suffered an accident while riding from his home to a store. Even though all riding was done with parental consent and the student had arrived home safely first, the parents sued.

Being in the right or winning a lawsuit still subjects you to losing time, money and sleep. What would you have done in the foregoing case? Could you have avoided placing yourself in a damaging situation?

OUTSIDE EVENTS

Some teachers go out of their way to throw themselves into a lawsuit. One sixth-grade teacher was waving a ruler about during a class lecture in front of his classroom when he became the object of obscene remarks by two boys walking outside. He grabbed the boys and pulled them into a coatroom within the classroom where he could talk to them and still observe his class.

One of the boys lunged toward the door and collided with the teacher. Both fell to the floor. Later the boys accused the teacher of beating them with the ruler.

In a court trial, photographs of bruises on the boys were given as evidence. The teacher was judged guilty of battery, but an appeals court overruled the judgment in a split decision. Whether the teacher was guilty of beating the boys or of using poor judgment remains unclear. Either way, he undoubtedly suffered sleepless nights and loss of respect from pupils and peers. He also lost money.

STRIPPED OF DIGNITY

Three teachers should have known better when they searched 28 third-grade students because four dollars disappeared from a fund-raising kitty. The teachers herded the students, boys and girls, into restrooms and asked them to remove or lower at least part of their clothing. Such acts naturally cause embarrassment to children and ripples of anger in the community. The money was later found in a boy's locker.

In another case, a swimming class of boys was told to empty their pockets and have their wallets checked by the vice-principal after money was stolen. Then the vice-principal and a deputy sheriff had three boys, including the prime suspect, strip to their shorts. The suspect was told to remove his shorts and money was found hidden inside them.

An appeals court ruled that a "general exploratory search" of all students violated the constitutional rule that searches must be particular and specific and that "the nature of the offense and the lack of any need for swift action did not require the embarrassment and indignity to 14-year-olds necessarily involved in stripping them naked in front of their peers."

Would you be willing to go to court and/or lose your job over four dollars? No? Don't be too sure. You probably wouldn't strip-search a student, but you could make an equally rash decision when an item disappears from class. Things will be stolen from the classroom during your teaching career. Count on it. Think about possible actions you can take now. Don't wait until the stress of the moment when you won't be thinking clearly.

DO YOUR DUTY

One sure way to be sued is shirking your duty. As a teacher, you'll be assigned to supervise children at bus stops, during recess, at lunch time, during assemblies and at other gatherings. Be there. Be on time. Watch the children. Ignoring children while gabbing to a colleague is likely to place you on the wrong side of a lawsuit.

True, accidents can occur outside your field of vision while you're on playground duty. However, if you are walking in your assigned area, you are being reasonably watchful and it lets you off the hook. Sitting in your classroom when you are assigned to watching children outside does not let you off the hook. It puts you on the spot.

One teacher, engrossed in talking to a drop-in parent, forgot she was assigned to bus duty after school. A pupil grabbed the advantage of her absence to do silly, attention-gaining acts in front of his peers and ran into the side of a school bus as it pulled into the parking area. He gained his peers' attention, all right. The bus ran over his foot. The teacher was sued. She had little defense; she was not doing her duty.

IN QUANDARIES

Teachers dream of just being able to teach. It doesn't work that way around children. Events change so fast you'll be in a quandary countless times. You'll have to make snap decisions, knowing you won't always be right and recognizing that wrong decisions will throw you in hot water.

For instance, fighting among students is a common problem and you'll be first on the scene of several fights around school grounds during your career. It's only one test of your decision-making under duress.

Do you wade in between the combatants and force them apart? I wouldn't recommend this method even for a three-hundred-pound heavyweight. It's too easy to have a finger bent back or catch a swinging fist in the eye.

You could do a quick about-face and pretend you didn't notice the action. But do it, and you'll face the wrath of a principal, parents, and maybe a judge.

Your best decision would be to yell loudly as you approach. This usually stops the fighting because both pugilists are hoping they can quit without losing face. If your loud, authoritative bellow doesn't do the job, send for other teachers and an administrator for physical assistance. Knowing others are coming does much for cooling tempers. No matter what you do, keep in mind how frail a human body, yours, is and how eagerly parents respond to finding a teacher scapegoat for their children's misdeeds.

TRIPPING ON FIELD TRIPS

Field trips can be a lawyer's delight. Trips to the zoo, museum, or a tree farm call for many pairs of watchful eyes. This is true whether the pupils are in kindergarten or high school.

Always have a signed permission slip for each child. Take along another teacher or counselor, if possible. If not, include one or more parents. Parents have a tendency not to show up on occasion, so enlist the aid of several. Make their duties clear and assign them to watchful positions. You are in command; they just have to be alert.

I lost a junior high youngster on a field trip to Sea World. He deliberately hid when it was time for the bus's departure for school. We searched, of course, and then left him behind after telephoning his mother. It was a worrisome incident adding to my gray hairs. I hope you avoid such an experience.

I remember another youngster who, on a visit to a Christmas tree farm, discovered the only snake ever observed in wintertime on the farm. She was bitten when she picked it up. Thankfully, it wasn't a rattlesnake, and, fortunately, there was no lawsuit.

NEVER ASSUME

Beginning teachers are too trusting. I shuddered when I observed an inexperienced kindergarten teacher line up her charges, eyes to the front, and lead them three blocks to the county library. At intersections the children fended for themselves, dodging intermittent cars. Luckily, everyone reached the destination.

In her ignorance, the teacher didn't realize how easily negligence could have been proven in court had a child been injured. She should have enlisted the aid of several parents to herd the kindergarteners.

Never assume a child will behave as an adult would. On the other hand, some youngsters exhibit adult behavior in disastrous ways. I once unwisely dispatched a youngster to the office unescorted after he had caused several classroom disturbances. He arrived bloody and bruised with a story about my hitting him. The boy must have been in training for cheating insurance companies by jumping in front of automobiles because he had been observed scraping his face along the rough stucco walls of the school building while enroute to the office.

If he had not been observed, I could have been involved in legal action. I learned the hard way that a single, unimportant incident has nightmare possibilities.

READ ABOUT IT

Read the education code. It should be mandatory for teachers to be familiar with their state's education code. You can find a copy within the school district. Your principal probably has a copy in the office. Borrow it. It'll open your eyes. It'll also make you see how vulnerable you are.

Review recent books on school law. A useful monthly publication entitled *Your School and The Law* has brief synopses of court cases involving schools and teachers. It's sent to school superintendents, school board members, and principals. Your school district should have copies. If not, talk your principal into writing for copies from: Professional Publications, P.O. Box 80097, Atlanta, Georgia, 30341. Then borrow them.

California published an easily read, useful booklet entitled *Law In The School* and you might secure a copy by writing to: Patterson Smith Publishing Company, 23 Prospect Terrace, Montclair, New Jersey, 07042. Although it pertains to laws in California school situations, it is helpful because most school laws in other states are similar.

Another well-written book is *Law In The Schools* by William D. Valente and published by Charles E. Merrill Publishing Company. It covers all states and includes a list of addresses where you can write for the education codes of any state.

A CRIME IS A CRIME

Criminal laws of the nation and of states apply to schools. Stepping across a school boundary does not exempt one from laws nor does it eliminate one's rights.

Stealing is a crime and, even if it occurs on school property, police are allowed to investigate. Call for the principal if there's a theft in your classroom and you can't find the culprit immediately. The principal can then question students or ask for police assistance, if necessary. You check on the crime as much as possible, but don't assume the whole burden.

Some teachers have undertaken the Sherlock Holmes role much to their sorrow. Even knowing who the thief is doesn't always turn up stolen property and searching or accusing students can leave you at the wrong end of the law. Let your principal call in the police for anything serious. The police are better trained to find lawbreakers. Let them. Devote your time to educating children to be better citizens.

9 THE REWARDS

Perhaps, after reading this far, you're having second thoughts about becoming a teacher. I hope you don't do like two recent college graduates who read the unfinished manuscript of this book during its writing. Although they had completed all teaching credential requirements, both immediately sought positions in another field of work.

Don't let anything discussed in this book discourage you. If teaching is in your blood, you'll do great. Teaching, like every occupation, has its negative aspects and one purpose of this book is to give you a glimmer of what to expect, good or bad. This chapter will cover some of the better features and advantages in teaching.

STEADY AS CLOCKWORK

Money is the most obvious reward. Paychecks arrive regularly no matter how much the stock market goes up or down. Factories can close and throw people on unemployment lines, but you won't be among those having to miss mortgage payments.

True, other professions have higher salaries, but a teacher's pay is adequate. It'll buy your house and put shoes on the baby. It'll even let you tour Europe if you manage your money well.

However, there is an often overlooked, unpublicized salary fact. Although many people believe teachers are paid twelve months a year, they're not. Teachers are paid an annual salary based upon the number of months taught. Some school districts divide the total amount into ten equal monthly payments; some into twelve. Those teachers paid in

93

ten installments need to save for summer months when no paycheck arrives.

AN INNER GLOW

With many teachers, pay is secondary. Oh, they'll fight for better salaries every year, but if they really wanted big bucks, they would seek another profession.

For these teachers, the real payoff is personal gratification. They bask in the warm feeling derived from contributing to the welfare of children and attain a sense of well-being when children look to them for guidance. For some, perhaps, it's simply an enjoyment of being able to contribute to the field of knowledge.

Whatever your personal reasons for wanting to be a teacher, you'll have your peak moments; you'll have times when you'll positively glow with satisfaction and know your choice of professions was correct. At such moments you'll understand why so many teachers resist tempting offers to leave classrooms. These moments will overshadow your more erratic days.

THE DAWNING AND REMEMBRANCE

There will be times when, after your repeated frustrations trying to explain a simple process, a child's blank, bewildered countenance will blossom into a radiance of understanding. That sudden beaming of discovery always lightens the day and puts a spring into a teacher's walk.

There will also be times when you'll bask in prideful sunshine as poor readers begin frequenting libraries because your efforts spurred youngsters into higher achievement, and, also, you might experience times when children who have been rooted to desks in beet-faced shyness grow into confident classroom speakers under your leadership.

You'll have your moments in later years, too, when a former student recognizes you on the street and thanks you

94

for forcing him or her to learn, or when a parent requests that a son or daughter be placed in your room because the parent had learned so well as a youngster in your classroom.

Without question, moments of recognition are rare, but, as the years pass, thousands of adults will owe part of their awareness of life and knowledge to you. You will have increased their understanding, even though it remains buried in their subconsciousness, and to some teachers that is reward enough.

TIME OFF

While you're waiting for that inner glow of satisfaction, consider the more tangible benefits. No doubt you've already thought of teachers' long summer vacations. Few other occupations offer scheduled two-month vacations plus a two-week Christmas vacation and a spring vacation. In addition, teachers have most holidays others enjoy. Excluding summers, paychecks still arrive monthly. It's almost as good as being in Congress where members set their own vacations.

You'll need and look forward to all vacations because teaching is more exhausting and stressful than realized by the general public. Anyone not understanding the emotional strain resulting from being near restless children need only ask any parent with one or two children for opinions regarding child rearing, especially near the end of summer vacation. They have one or two; you'll face from twenty-five to two hundred children a day.

MOONLIGHTING

Teachers not blessed with a working spouse or extra income to tide them over payless summer months use summertime profitably for other employment. I recommend working even if you aren't short of funds. Experiencing different jobs expands your horizons and brings new meanings into your classroom exercises.

95

I've taught during summer school and greeted my September classes feeling totally exhausted. I've also worked as a forest ranger, campground inspector for a campground directory publisher, landscape gardener, painter, tree farmer, and in a variety of other jobs. All of these left me refreshed in September and contributed to my effectiveness as a teacher. They also contributed to my bank account.

EXOTIC PLACES

If you save your money or are independently wealthy, you can take extensive vacations during summers. Months of free time enable you to travel across the United States visiting relatives and still have time to tour the Greek Isles. Possibly, if you gather information helpful to your teaching, you can declare the travel as an income tax deduction. Get IRS approval first on this one because tax people are quick to disallow suspicious deductions. History teachers can justify visits to Rome easier than gym teachers.

THE OTHER SIDE OF THE DESK

You might also qualify for tax deductions by taking college courses to improve your teaching skills. Treasury regulations, which are always subject to change, permit an income tax deduction for educational expenses (registration fees, cost of travel, meals and lodging) undertaken to: (1) maintain or improve skills required in one's employment, or (2) meet express requirements of an employer or a law imposed as a condition to retention of employment, job status, or rate of compensation.

Aside from possible tax deductions, professional improvement has other rewards. School districts base pay scales on additional credits earned in college and for having advanced degrees as well as the number of years taught, so it pays to return to college for that M.A. degree. Attend classes connected to your teaching field because some districts are fussy. They might give an art teacher credit for an art course while refusing an English teacher credit for the same course.

No matter how exhausted teaching leaves you, and it will, it's money in your pocket if you force yourself to endure college evening classes. Attend Saturday classes if no local college is available and you must drive to another city. The faster you earn extra units of credit, the faster you advance on the pay scale.

You'll discover that some districts require continuing college attendance as a condition of employment. Even if your district does not, it still benefits you to add to your teaching knowledge.

THE FRINGE

Most workers take fringe benefits such as health plans and retirement plans for granted as an automatic part of the job. Don't. Fringe benefits didn't arrive as gifts to teachers. Thirty years ago they were nearly nonexistent in education and teachers now retired or among the older members of your staff fought for them one at a time.

Appreciate the benefits of medical plans or whatever additional benefits your district has because these hard-earned fringe benefits are among the first cost-cutting measures school board members examine. Sabbatical leave with pay falls first when school boards sharpen the ax, with automatic pay increases, district-paid dental plans, and health insurance not far behind.

It's been estimated that fringe benefits add nearly fifty percent more to an average worker's salary. In any case, they certainly are a hidden wage increase and, in addition, many of the benefits can free your mind from financial worries that might affect your teaching. A teacher fretting over a spouse's hospital bills isn't giving a school district one hundred percent on the job.

A LITTLE CREDIT

Beginning teachers usually don't consider credit unions as one of the teaching benefits. Some don't even know they exist.

Teachers do have and do belong to credit unions. State teacher organizations, county teacher organizations and local school districts have them. You will eventually join one.

I recall a newly-hired teacher whose first paycheck was delayed one month. Burdened with the expense of moving from another state, he ran out of money so he and his family were subsisting on popcorn when his plight was noticed. Informed of the credit union, he rushed to join and immediately borrowed against his missing check. His family ate steak that night.

Credit unions are handy whether you get into a financial bind or want to buy a fishing boat or a bulldozer. I've been able to borrow up to two thousand dollars at a low interest rate just by picking up the telephone. The check was in the mailbox the next day.

Credit unions now offer many banking services and are an excellent place to save money for payless summers. You can have automatic pay deductions sent by your school district directly to a credit union to even out your pay over twelve months. Generally, the interest paid on credit union deposits has been higher than interest paid by banks.

Wise teachers with money for a down payment on a house have deposited the money in their credit union and borrowed the down payment using their own money as collateral. They paid four percent more interest on the loan than they were paid for the deposit. What appears to be a losing financial deal isn't because interest payments paid on loan balances are lowered as monthly payments are made while interest paid by the credit union is paid on the entire amount of deposit. Eventually, more interest is earned than paid and the original deposit still remains intact.

THE SEVEN-YEAR ITCH

It's said that the average family moves every seven years. You might be one of those who finds a niche and drops anchor permanently. Then again, you might be one who says, "Hey, I can get a job teaching anywhere if I want to move."

Maybe you can. Teaching positions are found in all parts of the United States and many foreign countries. In normal times teachers can secure teaching positions in other cities when their spouse is transferred, or if they feel they've been in a place so long they're growing moss. Don't wait too long to make your move if you plan to switch areas. Most districts allow credit for previous teaching experience for payroll purposes, but they generally have a cut-off time of from three to five years. Wait too long and you'll lose money.

You don't have to be stuck in a ghetto school forever just because that was your only job offer when you started. There are schools surrounded by green grass and blue skies if that's your preference.

Choose areas of your choice and send for application blanks. Hawaii, Alaska, Montana, or Saudi Arabia have schools, too. That's right—Saudi Arabia. American firms and the United States government operate schools in foreign countries for the children of employees. Get in touch with the firm or government agency for information about specific openings. Some teachers prefer to teach overseas. It's a change of pace.

TENURE

Most teachers remain in one district until they retire. An advantage of staying in one district, besides the obvious one of not starting over near the bottom of the pay scale, is tenure. Tenure is job security to protect the teacher from outside pressure or from school boards that fire teachers and replace them with lower-paid, inexperienced people to save money. It is not a job guarantee as some citizens think. Teachers can be dismissed, but it's a more involved process than simply saying, "You're fired."

Generally, teachers can be dismissed after being given written notice and having a hearing before the school board for any of the following reasons:

1. Immoral or unprofessional conduct.
2. Doing or advocating the commission of acts of criminal syndicalism (illegal strikes).
3. Dishonesty.
4. Incompetency.
5. Evident unfitness for service.
6. Physical or mental condition unfitting one to instruct or associate with children.
7. Persistent violation of or refusal to obey the school laws of the state or reasonable regulations prescribed by the State Board of Education or governing board of the school district.
8. Conviction of a felony or of any crime involving moral turpitude.
9. Membership in the Communist Party.

EASE OF MIND

Reasons for dismissal are so wide-ranging and so vague they can be used to dismiss any teacher. Fortunately, any teacher about to be fired is entitled to a hearing and can appeal an unfavorable decision to the proper court. Unfortunately, some districts keep incompetent teachers to avoid the bother of gathering information for a court case, much to the distress of better teachers.

The benefit of tenure comes not in having a lifelong teaching position, but in knowing that no administrator will drop into your room late Friday and hand you a pink slip denoting dismissal. Factory workers seldom have such job security.

You can't be easily dismissed simply to make room for someone's friend or because you angered the PTA president. However, you can be dismissed if the district enrollment drops and the teaching staff is cut, but, even then, your job continues until the end of the school year because teachers are employed on a yearly basis.

As you stay in one district, you gain seniority. The old saying, "Last hired, first fired," works in education, too. Tenure laws permit you to gain that seniority.

EQUAL RIGHTS

Nationwide women earn less than men. In fact, male high school graduates stand to earn more in a lifetime than most female university graduates.

In educational fields women are on equal footing with their male colleagues and teaching attracts some women mainly for this reason. As men strive for higher salaries they garner equally high salaries for all female members of the staff. Thus, it becomes a team effort to better salaries and conditions.

Women are more apt to be in administrative positions, especially at the principal level, than in many occupations, but prejudice still exists. Few women are found as district superintendents or assistant superintendents. Any woman desiring to run a public school district will find it easier to be elected to the school board than to be selected as the superintendent.

STAGE FRIGHT

An often overlooked aspect of teaching is the tremendous boosting of confidence. Directing your own successful activities does wonders for ego strength and few people who remain under constant scrutiny by children are going to retain any natural shyness.

Teachers who actually became ill when giving talks in college classes have stood before audiences of parents in packed auditoriums and introduced school plays without an outward flutter.

You don't think you can do it? You'll be surprised. It sort of sneaks up on you.

There's a carryover value to this confidence building. It's easier to obtain other employment, either during summer months or permanently. Employers welcome persons who have the ability to speak easily and intelligently on a wide range of subjects to a wide variety of people. If you are still attending college, take as many courses outside the education field as you can so you can cash in on potential occupational opportunities later.

BEING SHIFTY

Another teaching benefit is being able to change jobs while doing the same thing. Confusing? Not really.

Suppose you begin teaching in a primary class and don't feel at ease with small children or you teach junior high mathematics and hate it. Are you stuck in that position? You don't have to be. Simply shift to another subject or class level. Ask to be considered for a different position and you'll be transferred if there's an opening and if your seniority precludes someone else's getting the job first. Teachers frequently shift from school to school or from one class to another. As long as it's within one district, there's no loss of pay or fringe benefits.

THE COMPANY YOU KEEP

You might or might not consider being around other teachers a blessing, but it is a subtle benefit of teaching.

Teachers as a group are fascinating. Step into any workroom and listen to the conversation. Sure, you'll hear gripes about the job and the usual Monday morning sports roundup, but you'll also overhear knowledgeable discussions on a wide range of topics. Few groups keep abreast of events and pursue information as teachers do.

Teachers involve themselves in hobbies, travel, education, politics, community affairs, financial matters, and religion. They like to debate, discuss, or joke among themselves about any of their interests. You'll enjoy being part of the group. Most likely, you'll join right in and yack it up with them.

ON YOUR SHOULDERS

This book is intended to open only one window in the field of teaching because it's impossible to cover everything you will encounter from day to day. Even as you teach, you won't know what to expect from moment to moment. That's what makes teaching exciting.

A heavy responsibility will rest on your shoulders should you become a teacher, but feel confident that you are up to the challenge. You must have given some thought to teaching before you decided to devote a minimum of four years in college readying yourself for the position. Possibly, you have the makings of one of the great teachers of your generation. Go ahead. Go out and launch your career.

APPENDIX

Teachers need access to an astonishing amount of knowledge covering a wide range of subjects. The following organizations can provide more detailed information about a specific interest area or topic. Most have a public relations person who will furnish needed data or guide you to the correct source.

NATIONAL EDUCATIONAL ORGANIZATIONS

National Education Association (NEA), 1201 16th Street NW, Washington, D.C., 20036   (202) 833-4484

American Federation of Teachers (AFT), 11 DuPont Circle NW, Washington, D.C., 20036   (202) 797-4400

(Both organizations have material about the teaching field in general)

UNITED STATES GOVERNMENT

Teacher Exchange Section, International Exchange Branch, Division of International Education, Department of Education, 7th and D Streets SW, ROB3, Room 3068, Washington, D.C. 20202 (202)245-2454 (Information on swapping teaching positions with a teacher in a foreign country)

Women's Program Staff, Department of Education, 400 Maryland Avenue SW, Donohoe Building, Room 1100, Washington, D.C., 20202   (202) 245-2181 (Provides grants for the improvement and expansion of innovative programs by women)

Guaranteed Student Loan Branch, Division of Policy and Program Development, Bureau of Student Financial Assistance, Department of Education, ROB3, Room 4310, Washington, D.C., 20202   (202) 245-9717 (Authorizes low-interest loans of from $2,500 to $15,000 to eligible college students)

Student Information, Department of Education, 7th and D Streets SW, Washington, D.C., 20202   (800) 638-6700, in Maryland (800) 492-6602   (A toll-free hotline to provide the latest information regarding federally funded loan and grant programs to assist students in continuing their education)

Office of Public Affairs, Department of Education, 400 Maryland Avenue SW, Room 2089, Washington, D.C., 20202 (202)245-8564 (Provides a free directory of publications from the Department of Education)

Peace Corps, ACTION, Room M-1200, 806 Connecticut Avenue NW, Washington, D.C., 20525   (202) 254-7970 (For information and the nearest recruiting office for teachers desiring to work two years in another country in the Peace Corps)

Publications, Public Communications, Small Business Administration, 1441 L Street NW, Room 100, Washington, D.C., 20416 (800) 433-7212, in Texas   (800) 792-8901 (A toll-free number for free publications about retail and service firms)

Superintendent of Documents, Government Printing Office, Washington, D.C., 20402   (202) 783-3238 (Ask for a copy of "Just for You," an illustrated and annotated catalog of publications covering a wide range of topics. Other publications are also available)

Office of Public Programs, Bureau of Public Affairs, Department of State, 2201 C Street NW, Room 5825, Washington, D.C., 20520   (202) 632-1433 (U.S. Department of State officers are available to speak to institutions and groups throughout the country)

Photo Library, Office of Public Affairs, National Park Service, Department of the Interior, Room 3043, Washington, D.C., 20240   (202) 523-0051 (Prints and transparencies can be borrowed free of charge on all aspects of the National Parks including natural history and geologic features)

Office of Public Affairs, National Park Service, Department of the Interior, Room 3043, Washington, D.C., 20240   (202) 343-7394 (Ask for a list of publications covering the 290 areas administered by the National Park Service)

National Cartographic Information Center, National Mapping Division, Geological Survey, Department of the Interior, 507 National Center, Reston, Virginia, 22092 (703)860-6045 (Detailed aerial photographs of almost any neighborhood in the U.S.A. can be purchased for a small fee)

Public Information Division, NIH, Department of Health and Human Services, Room 305, Bethesda, Maryland, 20205 (301) 496-4143 (A free catalogue of health publications is available)

Resort Guides, National Oceanographic Data Center, EDIS/NOAA, Department of Commerce, Room 428 Page 1, Washington, D.C., 20235   (202) 634-7506 (Free resort guides for various parts of the United States are available)

Public Affairs Office, NOAA, Department of Commerce, 30 Marine Street, Boulder, Colorado, 80302   (303) 499-1000 (Provides information on upper atmosphere, space, and interactions of the sun and earth)

Reference Section, National Audiovisual Center, National Archives and Records Service, General Services Administration, Washington, D.C., 20409   (301)763-1896 (Ask for the free catalog, "A Reference List of Audiovisual Materials Produced by the U.S. Government," for AV materials regarding military matters)

107

Publications and Visual Aids Branch, Operations and Services Division, Office of Management Systems, Federal Highway Division, Department of Transportation, 400 7th Street S.W., Room 6415, Washington, D.C., 20590   (202) 426-0473 (Ask for a description of films available on a free loan basis)

Community and Educational Services Branch, Public Affairs Division, National Aeronautics and Space Administration, 400 Maryland Ave. S.W., Room F6052, Washington, D.C, 20546   (202)755-3350 (Has a free quarterly report for elementary and secondary educators)

Office of Elementary and Secondary Education, Smithsonian Institution, 900 Jefferson Drive S.W., Washington, D.C., 20560   (202) 357-2425 (Ask for "Art to 200," a newsletter for teachers from 4th to 8th grades, and "Learning Opportunities" for information on programs available to schools)

Photographic Services, Smithsonian Institution, 1000 Jefferson Drive S.W., Washington, D.C., 20560   (202) 357-1487 (Ask for information, order forms and price lists of photographs of the many Smithsonian collections and from the photographic archives)

REGIONAL DEPOSITORY LIBRARIES

The following libraries have been designated as regional depository libraries and are required to receive and retain a copy of every publication by the United State government. They are a good reference source, but be specific in any request for information.

Auburn University of Montgomery Library, Montgomery, Alabama

University of Alabama Library, University, Alabama

Department of Library and Archives, Phoenix, Arizona

University of Arizona Library, Tucson, Arizona

California State Library, Sacramento, California

University of Colorado Libraries, Boulder, Colorado

Denver Public Library, Denver, Colorado

Connecticut State Library, Hartford, Connecticut

University of Florida Libraries, Gainesville, Florida

University of Idaho Library, Moscow, Idaho

Illinois State Library, Springfield, Illinois

Indiana State Library, Indianapolis, Indiana

University of Iowa, Iowa City, Iowa

Watson Library, University of Kansas, Lawrence, Kansas

Margaret I. King Library, University of Kentucky, Lexington, Kentucky

Louisiana State University Library, Baton Rouge, Louisiana

Louisiana Technical University Library, Ruston, Louisiana

Raymond H. Fogler Library, University of Maine, Portland, Maine

McKeldin Library, University of Maryland, College Park, Maryland

Boston Public Library, Boston, Massachusetts

Detroit Public Library, Detroit, Michigan

Michigan State Library, Lansing, Michigan

Wilson Library, University of Minnesota, Moorhead, Minnesota

University of Mississippi Library, University, Mississippi

University of Montana Library, Missoula, Montana

Nebraska Publications Clearinghouse, Nebraska Publications Commission, Lincoln, Nebraska

University of Nevada, Reno, Nevada

Newark Public Library, Newark, New Jersey

Zimmerman Library, University of New Mexico, Albuquerque, New Mexico

New Mexico State Library, Santa Fe, New Mexico

New York State Library, Albany, New York

University of North Carolina Library, Chapel Hill, North Carolina

North Dakota State Library, Fargo, North Dakota

Ohio State Library, Columbus, Ohio

Oklahoma Department of Libraries, Oklahoma City, Oklahoma

Portland State University Library, Portland, Oregon

State Library of Pennsylvania, Harrisburg, Pennsylvania

Texas State Library, Austin, Texas

Merrill Library and Learning Resources Center, Utah State University Library, Logan, Utah

Alderman Library, University of Virginia, Charlottesville, Virginia

Washington State Library, Olympia, Washington

West Virginia University Library, Morgantown, West Virginia

State Historical Society Library, Madison, Wisconsin

Milwaukee Public Library, Milwaukee, Wisconsin

Wyoming State Library, Laramie, Wyoming

FOREIGN COUNTRIES

Australian Tourist Commission, 1270 Avenue of the Americas, #2908, New York, NY 10020 (Information covers travel, recreation, and visitor attractions)

Tourism, Government of the Province of British Columbia, 1117 Wharf St., Victoria, British Columbia, Canada V8W2Z2 (Travel features on British Columbia)

Chinese Information Service, 159 Lexington Avenue, New York, NY 10016 (Pamphlets on art, music, and history of China)

Finland National Tourist Office, 75 Rockefeller Plaza, New York, NY, 10019 (Offers information on art, history, nature, sports, and travel)

Icelandic National Tourist Office, 75 Rockefeller Plaza, New York, NY 10019 (Publications include "Some Facts on Iceland," "Iceland Awaits You," "Practical Tourist Information," and "Country and People")

Italian Government Travel Office, 630 5th Avenue, New York, NY 10021 (brochures, pamphlets, and maps)

Panama Canal Information Office, Box M, Balboa Heights, Canal Zone (Information on the history, operation, and maintenance of the waterway)

Puerto Rico Tourism Company, 1290 Avenue of the Americas, New York, NY 10019 (Brochures and pamphlets)

Venezuelan Government Tourist and Information Center, 450 Park Avenue, New York, NY 10022 (Ask for the publication, "Venezuela A to Z")